Time Out

LONDON
TOP 100

www.timeout.com

Time Out Digital Ltd
4th Floor
125 Shaftesbury Avenue
London WC2H 8AD
Tel: + 44 (0)20 7813 3000
Email: guides@timeout.com
www.timeout.com

Published by Time Out Digital Ltd, a wholly owned subsidiary of Time Out Group Ltd.
Time Out and the Time Out logo are trademarks of Time Out Group Ltd.

© **Time Out Group Ltd 2015**
Previous editions 2011, 2013.

10 9 8 7 6 5 4 3 2 1

This edition first published in Great Britain in 2015 by Ebury Publishing
20 Vauxhall Bridge Road, London SW1V 2SA

Ebury Publishing is part of the Penguin Random House group of companies whose addresses
can be found at global.penguinrandomhouse.com

Distributed in the US and Latin America by Publishers Group West (1-510-809-3700)

For further distribution details, see www.timeout.com

ISBN: 978-1-90504-293-7

A CIP catalogue record for this book is available from the British Library.

Printed and bound in China by Leo Paper Products Ltd.

Penguin Random House is committed to a sustainable future for our business, our readers and
our planet. This book is made from Forest Stewardship Council® certified paper.

MIX
Paper from
responsible sources
FSC® C018179

EDITORIAL
Editor Elizabeth Winding
Deputy Editor Cath Phillips
Listings Editor William Crow
Proofreader John Shandy Watson

Editorial Director Sarah Guy
Group Finance Manager Margaret Wright

DESIGN
Senior Designer Kei Ishimaru
Group Commercial Senior Designer Jason Tansley

PICTURE DESK
Picture Editor Jael Marschner
Deputy Picture Editor Ben Rowe
Picture Researcher Lizzy Owen

ADVERTISING
Managing Director St John Betteridge
Advertising Sales Deborah Maclaren, Helen Debenham @ The Media Sales House

MARKETING
Senior Publishing Brand Manager Luthfa Begum
Head of Circulation Dan Collins

PRODUCTION
Production Controller Katie Mulhern

TIME OUT GROUP
Chairman & Founder Tony Elliott
Chief Executive Officer Tim Arthur
Chief Financial Officer Matt White
Publisher Alex Batho

CONTRIBUTORS
The Editor would like to thank Tania Ballantine, Matthew Bremner, Simon Coppock, Guy Dimond, Katie Dailey, Richard Ehrlich, Tristran Parker, Holly Pick, and all contributors to the *Time Out London* guide and *1000 things to do in London*, whose work forms the basis for parts of this book.

MAPS
JS Graphics (john@jsgraphics.co.uk).

PHOTOGRAPHY pages 3 Alessandro Colle/Shutterstock.com; 6 (bottom left), 41 (left and top right), 44, 92/93, 118 (left), 144, 145 Michelle Grant; 6 (right) Giovanni G/Shutterstock.com; 6 (middle right), 136/137 Clare Skinner; 6 (bottom right), 107 (top right and bottom right) Elisabeth Blanchet; 7 (top left) Rama Knight/Wellcome Images; 7 (middle left), 113 IR Stone/Shutterstock.com; 7 (bottom left) Jael Marschner; 7 (top right), 15, 24 (right), 58 (top), 74 (top left, top right and bottom right), 79, 80, 100/101, 106, 116, 126 (top), 132, 141 (bottom) Jonathan Perugia; 7 (bottom right), 19 John Holdship; 9 (top left) ©ZSL; 9 (bottom left), 17 (bottom right), 22/23, 122 (top left, bottom left and top right) Heloise Bergman; 9 (top right) Melvyn Vincent; 9 (middle right), 31 (top right), 38 Alys Tomlinson; 11, 107 (top left) Ed Marshall; 12/13 Giles Barnard; 14 Lance Bellers/Shutterstock.com; 16, 52, 77, 84, 88, 91 (top left), 143 Ben Rowe; 17 (top left), 102 (bottom right) Christina Theisen; 17 (bottom left) Heather Shaw; 17 (top right) David Axelbank; 18 (top left), 24 (top left and bottom left), 36/37 Britta Jaschinski; 18 (top right, bottom left and bottom right), 47 (middle left and bottom left), 53, 56, 69 (top left and bottom left), 74 (bottom left), 102 (left), 135, 146 Rob Greig; 20 RS Photography; 21 (left) Neil Lang/Shutterstock.com; 21 (top and bottom right), 49 (middle right), 139 (top) Ron Ellis/Shutterstock.com; 26, 54/55 Olivia Rutherford; 27 Charlie Hopkinson; 29 (top) vision7media; 29 (bottom left and bottom right) Mark Storey; 30 Clive Brunskill/Getty Images; 31 (top left, bottom left and bottom right), 62, 130 (top right and bottom right) Tove K Breitstein; 34 John Sturrock; 41 (bottom right) Mathew Greer; 42/43 Oliver Knight; 45 (left) johnbraid/Shutterstock.com; 45 (right) olling/Shutterstock.com; 47 (top left) SimonPRBenson/Shutterstock.com; 47 (top right and bottom right), 96, 107 (bottom left) Ming Tang-Evans; 47 (middle right), 85 (main and right), 94/95, 102 (top right), 117 Andrew Brackenbury; 48, 49 (top right and bottom), 50/51, 82/83, 140 Simon Leigh; 49 (top left), 152 (top right, bottom left and bottom right) Scott Wishart; 58 (bottom) Sir John Soane's Museum; 59, 114/115 © Museum of London; 63 Philip Vile; 64 (top left and bottom right) Pedro Rufo/Shutterstock.com; 64 (bottom left) astudio/Shutterstock.com; 64 (top right) Nando Machado/Shutterstock.com; 65 Will Rodrigues/Shutterstock.com; 66 mary416/Shutterstock.com; 67 (top) James Linsell-Clark; 67 (middle) Adam Gray; 67 (bottom left) © Her Majesty Queen Elizabeth II 2013; 68 chrisdorney/Shutterstock.com; 69 (right) Nigel Tradewell; 70 Anthony Webb; 71 Baloncici/Shutterstock.com; 72/73 © By kind permission of the Trustees of the Wallace Collection; 76 anyaivanova/Shutterstock.com; 78 (bottom left) Elena Dijour/Shutterstock.com; 78 (top right) Katy Peters; 81, 118 (right) Abigail Lelliott; 85 (left) Susannah Stone; 86/87 Giles Barnard; 90 Tricia De Courcy Ling; 91 (top left), 148/149 Piers Allardyce; 91 (bottom) pablo/Shutterstock.com; 97 (top right) Paul Winch-Furness; 97 (bottom left and bottom right) Sim Canetty-Clarke; 98 TTstudio/Shutterstock.com; 103 ©IWM; 104/105 Andrew Barker/Shutterstock.com; 108/109 Rafael Russell/Shutterstock.com; 111 Paul Grundy; 119 Thomas Owen Jenkins/Shutterstock.com; 120 Alexander Chaikin/Shutterstock.com; 121 Cedric Weber/Shutterstock.com; 122 (bottom right), 142 Alastair Muir; 123 ©Aki-Pekka Sinikoski; 124/125 Leon Chew; 128/129 cristapper/Shutterstock.com; 130 (left) Michael Franke; 133 (top and bottom) Pantelis Petrou; 133 (middle) Dominic Dorin; 134 Royal Academy of Arts; 138 (top) olavs/Shutterstock.com; 138 (bottom) Derry Moore; 139 (bottom) Emma Wood; 141 (top), 152 (top left) Nick Ballon; 150/151 Belinda Lawley; 153 Linus Lim

The following images were supplied by the featured establishments: pages 6 (top left), 9 (bottom right), 28, 32/33, 35, 39, 40, 57, 60/61, 67 (bottom right), 89, 97 (top left), 99, 110, 126 (middle and bottom), 127, 131, 147

Cover Photography: anyaivanova/Shutterstock.com

Introduction

There has never been a better time to visit the UK's capital: now, more than ever before, visitors are spoilt for choice when it comes to deciding what to see and do.

To help you choose, *London Top 100* is Time Out's pick of the city's finest attractions, taking in museums, markets, galleries, shops, sporting attractions, city farms, parks, pubs, restaurants, bars and clubs – not to mention a whole host of London icons, from the scarlet-clad guards of Buckingham Palace to the much-loved British Museum. Whether you're into the chic shops of Marylebone or the stalls of Spitalfields Market, afternoon tea at the Wolseley or a slice of London's nightlife, we've got it covered.

GETTING AROUND
The back of the book contains street maps of central London, starting on p154. The majority of our top 100 sights and attractions are marked on the maps, with a key on p157.

THE LISTINGS
While every effort has been made to ensure the accuracy of the information contained in this guide, the publishers cannot accept responsibility for any errors it may contain. Businesses can change their arrangements at any time, and it is always advisable to phone ahead to find out opening hours, prices and other particulars.

TELEPHONE NUMBERS
All telephone numbers listed in this guide assume that you are calling from within London. If you're ringing from outside the city, you will need to use the area code (020) before the phone number. If you're calling from abroad, dial your international access code or a '+', then 44 for the UK; follow that with 20 for London, then the eight-digit number.

WHAT DO YOU THINK?
We welcome feedback on all of our guides, so please email any comments or suggestions you may have to guides@timeout.com.

Best for...

A BIRD'S-EYE VIEW OF LONDON
Monument; no.23
The Shard; no.24
London Eye; no.49 ▶
Tower Bridge; no.50
Westminster Cathedral; no.60

LAZY SUNDAYS
BFI Southbank; no.18
Spitalfields & Brick Lane; no.47
Royal Botanic Gardens
  (Kew Gardens); no.57
Eat at a gastropub; no.85
Spend the day in Greenwich; no.91
◀ Columbia Road Market; no.97

SPORTS FANS
Queen Elizabeth Olympic Park; no.7
Wimbledon; no.13
The O2; no.42
Wembley Stadium; no.65
Lord's Cricket Ground; no.88 ▶

ENTERTAINING THE KIDS
London Dungeon; no.17
◀ Science Museum; no.46
HMS Belfast; no.52
Hyde Park & Kensington Gardens;
  no.53
City Farms; no.63
Natural History Museum; no.83

FINDING A BARGAIN
Topshop; no.29
Camden Market; no.37
Spitalfields & Brick Lane; no.47
Eat well for less; no.59
Portobello Market; no.67 ▶
Shakespeare's Globe; no.99

QUIRKY COLLECTIONS
Horniman Museum; no.14
Sir John Soane's Museum; no.32
Old Operating Theatre, Museum
  & Herb Garret; no.35
Hunterian Museum; no.74
Ripley's Believe It or Not!; no.84
◄ Wellcome Collection; no.96

ICONIC LONDON EXPERIENCES
Walk the Thames Path; no.26
Saunter through Soho; no.56
Ride the Routemaster; no.62
Horse Guards Parade & the
  Changing the Guard; no.77
Trafalgar Square; no.82 ►
Buckingham Palace & the Royal
  Mews; no.89

RAINY AFTERNOONS
◄ Victoria & Albert Museum;
  no.3
British Museum; no.9
Museum of London; no.33
Imperial War Museum; no.64
Hampton Court Palace; no.68
Wellcome Collection; no.96

A TASTE OF LONDON LIFE
Borough Market; no.5 ►
Take afternoon tea; no 20
Chinatown; no.25
Sample the best of British;
  no.31
Eat at a gastropub; no.85

A MOMENT OF CALM
Chelsea Physic Garden; no.11
Dulwich Picture Gallery; no.34
Wallace Collection; no.43
Have a pint; no.44
Geffrye Museum; no.54
◄ Highgate Cemetery; no.87

THE DECADE
OF DECADENCE

Enter a golden age as you indulge in the glamour of
the 1930s, at one of England's finest Art Deco homes.

ENGLISH HERITAGE

ELTHAM PALACE
& GARDENS

Step into England's story

SERIOUS SHOPPING

Hit the shops in Marylebone; no.19
Topshop; no.29 ▶
Spitalfields & Brick Lane; no.47
Westfield London; no.55
Splash out at London's department stores; no.71

WILDLIFE & NATURE LOVERS

St James's Park; no.1
◀ ZSL London Zoo; no.4
WWT London Wetland Centre; no.48
Royal Botanic Gardens (Kew Gardens); no.57
Sea Life London Aquarium; no.95

URBAN SOPHISTICATES

Wigmore Hall; no 10
Take afternoon tea; no.20
Fortnum & Mason; no.41
Splash out at London's department stores; no.71
Sip a cocktail; no.94 ▶

ART APPRECIATION

◀ National Portrait Gallery; no.8
Whitechapel Gallery; no.21
Somerset House; no.27
National Gallery; no.58
The Tates; no.75
Royal Academy of Arts; no.86
Saatchi Gallery; no.90

A TOP NIGHT OUT

Comedy Store; no.6
Go clubbing; no.12 ▶
National Theatre; no.36
Sample the Camden scene; no.81
See a West End show; no.92
Sip a cocktail; no.94

London
Top 100

1 St James's Park

The most central Royal Park is also one of London's most charming green spaces. St James's Park (www.royalparks.org.uk) may be small, but the waterfowl lake that runs through its centre is a source of endless delight, with its splay-footed, barking coots and a colony of mischievous pelicans. A few years ago, one of the pelicans was caught on camera as it swallowed a passing pigeon; in general, though, the birds stick to a diet of fresh fish. If you want to see them gulping their lunch down, feeding time is at around 2.30pm daily.

Buckingham Palace overlooks the western edge of the park, and Horse Guards Parade opens up to the east. Between them, **Inn The Park** (7451 9999, www.peytonandbyrne.co.uk) is a well-sited, all-day eaterie; breakfast on buttermilk pancakes on the terrace, pop into the self-service café for lunch, or dine on seasonal British dishes in the restaurant.

2 | Tower of London

The Tower's craggy walls guard all sorts of grisly delights, from displays showing the gruesome ends of traitors, to the Royal Armouries' swords, poleaxes, morning stars (spiky maces) and cannons. The Yeoman Warders – popularly known as Beefeaters – have lurid tales to tell on their free, hour-long tours too. Less bloodthirsty visitors can admire the glittering Crown Jewels (get there early to avoid long queues) and the beautiful Medieval Palace, with its reconstructed bedroom, throne room and tranquil private chapel.

Tower Hill, EC3N 4AB (0844 482 7777, www.hrp.org.uk).
Tower Hill tube or Tower Gateway DLR.

3 Victoria & Albert Museum

Behind the V&A's imposing exterior lie seven floors of treasures that span the worlds of art, design, fashion, jewellery, photography, theatre, textiles and architecture, drawn from across the globe and down the ages. From benign-faced Buddhas to a life-size automated man-eating tiger, architectural drawings to monumental plaster casts of towering ancient columns, the collections are as varied as they are magnificent.

Highlights include the seven Raphael Cartoons, painted in 1515 as tapestry designs for the Sistine Chapel, and the gorgeous 16th-century Ardabil carpet, the world's oldest floor covering. Newly reopened is the Weston Cast Court with its wonderful Victorian plaster reproductions of famous monuments, including a 16-foot-tall copy of Michelangelo's *David*.

For advice on how best to negotiate the museum's riches, consult the ever-patient staff, who wield a formidable combination of leaflets, gallery floorplans, general knowledge and polite concern. And if it all becomes too much, stop for a breather in the lovely Victorian refreshment rooms.

Cromwell Road, SW7 2RL (7942 2000, www.vam.ac.uk). South Kensington tube.
▶ *For a fresh perspective on the collections – and a glass of wine – head to one of the V&A's brilliant Friday Late events; see no.72.*

Inquisitive monkeys, gorgeously patterned pythons and spindly stick insects – London Zoo has something for everyone. Penguin Beach, the Sumatran tiger cubs in Tiger Territory and, right by the main entrance, Gorilla Kingdom are all on the must-do list, but the meerkats, lemurs and giant anteaters are hard to resist too. A packed programme of live animal events keeps the kids entertained, whether it be a hands-on encounter with a bird-eating spider in BUGS, or an opportunity to admire prodigiously digging aardvarks in Animal Adventure, the children's zoo. *Regent's Park, NW1 4RY (7449 6200, www.zsl.org). Baker Street tube, or Camden tube then bus 274, C2.*

Temptation is all around at this sprawling food market: head out hungry to take advantage of abundant free samples of rare-breed charcuterie and fine cheeses, fragrant olive oils, cakes and pies. Highlights might include Spanish specialist Brindisa's chorizo and rocket rolls, Cannon and Cannon's artisanal British cured meats and Kappacasein's amazing toasted cheese sarnies – Montgomery cheddar, onions, leeks, garlic and Poilâne sourdough bread. The hordes descend on Saturdays; to avoid the crush, visit on Thursday or Friday afternoon.

Southwark Street, SE1 (7407 1002, www.boroughmarket.org.uk). London Bridge tube/rail.

6 Comedy Store

Born during the 1980s 'alternative comedy' boom, the daddy of UK comedy clubs attracts the sharpest, savviest comics on the circuit. For script-free sketches and surreal flights of fancy, you can't beat the twice-weekly improvised performances from the resident Comedy Store Players, featuring some of the UK's finest stand-ups. Those who like their comedy with a whiff of terror will relish the King Gong night, on the last Monday of the month, when would-be comics are given as much time on the stage as the rowdy audience will allow – barely time for a one-liner for some sorry souls.

1A Oxendon Street, SW1Y 4EE (0844 871 7699, www.the comedystore.co.uk). Leicester Square or Piccadilly Circus tube.

7 Queen Elizabeth Olympic Park

After a major revamp, the Olympic Park in Stratford, east London is now open to the public – and there's loads on offer. The wave-shaped Aquatics Centre is open for swimming and diving sessions, while the VeloPark is the place for cyclists of all persuasions, be it road, track, BMX or mountain biking. You can just turn up and play at the Lee Valley Hockey & Tennis Centre, although it might be advisable to book ahead. There are also acres of immaculate parkland and waterways, some inventive children's play areas, four walking trails, a couple dozen public artworks, plus the attraction of ascending the red squiggly tower that is the ArcelorMittal Orbit (pictured below left). The Olympic Stadium itself becomes the new home of West Ham football club (from 2016), but will also be used for major athletics, rugby and other sporting championships.

For more information, including festivals and other special events, check out the park's website.

www.queenelizabetholympicpark.co.uk.

8 National Portrait Gallery

The collection at the National Portrait Gallery celebrates the people who have helped to shape British life and culture since the early 16th century – who prove to be a fascinatingly motley crew. Here, you can meet the curious gaze of Sir Winston Churchill, make eyes at rosy-cheeked, saucily attired Nell Gwyn, mistress of Charles II, or watch a sleeping David Beckham, courtesy of artist Sam Taylor-Wood's oddly intimate video installation. The gallery starts with Tudor paintings on the second floor (the Chandos portrait of Shakespeare, Henry VIII by Holbein and the Ditchley Elizabeth I among them); as you approach the present day, the collection starts to include the familiar faces of contemporary sporting heroes, pop stars, actors, writers, politicians and artists. There are sculptures as well as paintings and photographs; in Room 38, you can't miss the bust of Marc Quinn, *Self*, made from the artist's own blood.
St Martin's Place, WC2H 0HE (7306 0055, www.npg.org.uk).
Leicester Square tube or Charing Cross tube/rail.

Open to 'studious and curious Persons' since it was founded in 1753, this is one of the greatest museums in the world. You could spend days exploring its amazing collections: highlights include the Parthenon sculptures and Rosetta Stone (left out of the main courtyard, if you enter via the main entrance), the Easter Island statue (ground floor, straight ahead) and the Egyptian mummies (upstairs, straight ahead). Upstairs, to the right, are the Lindow man, preserved in a peat bog right down to the bristles of his red beard, and the Sutton Hoo treasure hoard. At the museum's heart is the Great Court, now covered by a soaring glass and steel roof. The temporary exhibitions of treasures from around the globe are always interesting, often spectacular.

Great Russell Street, WC1B 3DG (7323 8299, www.british museum.org). Russell Square or Tottenham Court Road tube.

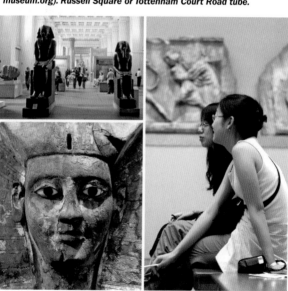

10 Wigmore Hall

Superb acoustics and a packed programme – over 400 events are held here each season – mean that the Wigmore, built in 1901, remains the grande dame of London's concert halls. It's an intimate place, with seating for fewer than 550 people. Chamber music (including new commissions) is the mainstay, but there's also a jazz programme, as well as all kinds of hands-on workshops and lively events for small fry. *36 Wigmore Street, W1U 2BP (7935 2141, www.wigmore-hall. org.uk). Bond Street tube.*

11 | Chelsea Physic Garden

Behind its high brick walls, the Chelsea Physic Garden is an oasis of green that has flourished on this site since 1673. The redesigned and replanted Garden of Medicinal Plants opened in 2014, bringing together plants that have been used in healing and medicine, sometimes for thousands of years, from every region of the world. Winter reveals a different aspect to the gardens, with banks of delicate snowdrops lending the place a magical, fairytale feel; afterwards, head to the café for a warming glass of mulled wine and a mince pie.

66 Royal Hospital Road, SW3 4HS (7352 5646, www.chelsea physicgarden.co.uk). Sloane Square tube or bus 11, 19, 170.

Much of London's nightlife is based in the east of the city. Top picks include **XOYO** (32-37 Cowper Street, EC2A 4AP, 7354 9993, www.xoyo. co.uk) in Shoreditch, and the **Nest** (36 Stoke Newington Road, N16 7XJ, 7354 9993, www.ilovethenest.com; pictured above) in Dalston, both of which provide cutting-edge house and cosmic disco for hip young things. On Kingsland High Street, **Dalston Superstore** (no.117, E8 2PB, 7254 2273, www.dalstonsuperstore.com) is popular with gay crowds and hosts edgy electro nights, while sister venue **Dance Tunnel** (no.95, E8 2PB, 7249 7865, www.dancetunnel.com) is a sweaty basement club that's perfect for heads-down raving to leftfield house heroes.

If you only visit one club in London, make it **Fabric** (77A Charterhouse Street, EC1M 6HJ, 7336 8898, www.fabriclondon.com), a cornerstone of London's nightlife scene for over a decade; world-class DJs put the

sublime sound system through its paces with drum 'n' bass and grime on Fridays, and hypnotic house and techno on Saturdays.

South of the Thames, the intimate **Corsica Studios** (4-5 Elephant Road, SE17 1LB, 7703 4760, www.corsicastudios.com) bulges with atmosphere and full-bodied techno, while the **CLF Art Café** (133 Rye Lane, SE15 4ST, 7732 5275, www.clfartcafe.org), inside multi-floored Peckham palace the Bussey Building, has an eclectic programme that traverses nu-disco, hip hop and even live funk at South London Soul Train. North Greenwich is rather out of the way, but **Studio 338** (338 Boord Street, SE10 0PF, 8293 6669, www.studio338.co.uk; pictured above) is worth the trip for dedicated dancers, who'll find one of the best club terraces in London, and DJs to match.

Vauxhall has long been a hedonistic hotspot for gay nightlife. The **Royal Vauxhall Tavern** (372 Kennington Lane, SE11 5HY, 7820 1222, www.rvt. org.uk) hosts wild performance/music mash-ups, while the welcoming Sunday-night parties from trendsetting DJ troupe Horse Meat Disco (pictured below) at **Eagle London** (349 Kennington Lane, SE11 5QY, 7793 0903, www.eaglelondon.com) are hugely popular.

13 Wimbledon

To see the world's leading tennis stars slogging it out on the courts, and indulge in the time-honoured strawberries and cream, Wimbledon (held over two weeks in late June and early July) is the place to be. Unusually for such a major sporting event, you can buy tickets on the day: the All England Club reserves around 500 tickets each for Centre Court and No.2 Court at the turnstiles daily from days one to nine of the tournament, while 500 tickets are available per day for No.1 Court for the entire 13 days. There's plenty of competition for the tickets, so expect to queue from very early in the morning – or even the night before. If you're unsuccessful, don't despair: several thousand ground admission tickets are also available at the gate throughout the tournament, although these don't give access to the show courts.

Open year-round, the **Wimbledon Lawn Tennis Museum** is a sleekly modern affair, where a hologram-like John McEnroe lurks in the 1980s Gentlemen's Dressing Room, reminiscing about old times, and an immersive cinema experience explores the science of the game.

All England Lawn Tennis Club, Church Road, SW19 5AE (8944 1066, www.wimbledon.com). Southfields tube or bus 493.

14 | Horniman Museum

Loved by locals, this one-of-a-kind museum was founded by Victorian tea trader Frederick J Horniman (and built by Charles Harrison Townsend, who also designed the Whitechapel Gallery; see no.21). African masks, Egyptian mummies and the famous stuffed walrus are among the quirky collection of artefacts and specimens from around the globe, along with 1,300 musical instruments in the revamped music gallery; use the touchscreen tables to unleash some weird and wonderful sounds. The basement aquarium is divided into seven different zones: look out for the strangely mesmerising moon jellyfish and the British seahorses.
***100 London Road, SE23 3PQ (8699 1872, www.horniman.ac.uk).
Forest Hill rail or bus 122, 176, 185, 363, P4, P13.***

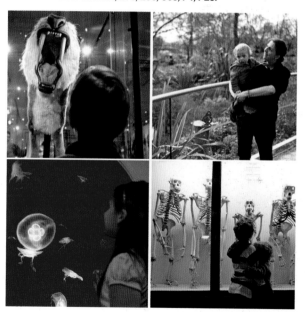

15 | Thames Clippers

As well as carrying suit-clad commuters up and down the Thames, Thames Clippers' fleet of high-speed catamarans is a brilliant way to see the sights. Services run all the way from Putney in the west, via the London Eye and both Tate galleries, to Greenwich and Woolwich in the east. Special 'River Roamer' tickets allow you to hop on and off all day. **0870 781 5049, www.thamesclippers.com.**
▶ *For a scenic journey back to central London, board a Clipper after a gig at the O2 arena; see no.42.*

16 Granary Square & the new King's Cross

The reinvention of the once-seedy King's Cross neighbourhood continues apace. It's got new buildings and streets, new homes and offices – even a brand-new London postcode: N1C.

St Pancras rail station has been reborn as the Eurostar terminus, combining Victorian grandeur with sleekly modern amenities. King's Cross station has also had its own smart makeover, and the land behind it has been turned into an impressive new public space, **Granary Square** (pictured). Here, you'll find the new home of Central Saint Martins art college and excellent places to eat – including restaurants Grain Store and Caravan, and Kerb's street-food traders, who turn up at weekday lunchtimes – as well as dancing fountains and assorted events. The latest arrival is the **House of Illustration** (3696 2020, www.houseofillustration.org.uk), encompassing political cartoons, animations and fashion design. Round the corner, the slick **Kings Place** development (90 York Way, N1 9AG, 7520 1490, www.kingsplace.co.uk) is known for its varied and inventive music gigs, plus debates and all manner of other delights. ***www.kingscross.co.uk.***

17 London Dungeon

Just across the River Thames from the Houses of Parliament, you'll find this gruesome romp through some of the darker episodes in the city's history. The Great Plague, Jack the Ripper, Bloody Mary and a blood-soaked operating theatre are among the attractions: expect a medley of hideous rotting corpses, boils, worm-filled skulls, scuttling rats, piercing screams and all-too-convincing actors, daubed with gore.

County Hall, Westminster Bridge Road, SE1 7PB (0871 423 2240, www.thedungeons.com). Waterloo tube/rail.

Welco
3 Ciner

BFI SOUTHBANK

Mediath
Gallery

Studio
Film

18 BFI Southbank

Beside the Thames, tucked underneath Waterloo Bridge, BFI Southbank
screens the broadest range of films in London. There are premières,
director Q&As, special seasons and interesting programming strands.
Meanwhile, pre-bookable viewing sessions in the Mediatheque offer
the chance to browse the BFI's vast archive, whose treasures run from
Edwardian clips of top-hatted gents crossing Blackfriars Bridge to *Monty
Python's Flying Circus* and 1950s Morris dancers.

For a larger-than-life cinematic experience and some spectacular 3D
screenings, head to the nearby **BFI IMAX** (1 Charlie Chaplin Walk, SE1
8XR, 0330 333 7878), whose screen is almost the height of five double-
decker buses.
South Bank, SE1 8XT (7928 3232, www.bfi.org.uk).
Embankment tube or Waterloo tube/rail.

19 Hit the shops in Marylebone

North of brash, busy Oxford Street, Marylebone is a polished enclave of upmarket shops. At its heart is Marylebone High Street, lined with chi-chi boutiques selling everything from cool Scandinavian homewares to exquisitely packaged chocolates and designer clothes. The Edwardian **Daunt Books** (no.83, W1U 4QW, 7224 2295, www.dauntbooks.co.uk; pictured bottom right) is London's loveliest bookshop, with its stained-glass windows and book-lined old oak galleries. As well as a stellar selection of cheese to buy, **La Fromagerie** (nos.2-6, W1U 4EW, 7935 0341, www.lafromagerie.co.uk) has a fine café, serving charcuterie, cheese and seasonal mains, along with divine cakes and hot chocolate.

Nearby Marylebone Lane is also dotted with gems. At **Tracey Neuls** (no.29, W1U 2NQ, 7935 0039, www.traceyneuls.com; pictured above), shoes are suspended from the ceiling like artworks, while famous haberdashery **VV Rouleaux** (no.102, W1U 2QD, 7224 5179, www.vvrouleaux.com) is a treasure trove of ribbons, trims and feathers, beloved by fashion stylists. **Content Beauty** (14 Bulstrode Street, W1U 2JG, 3075 1006, www.beingcontent.com) is perfect for niche, new and natural beauty brands. On Saturdays, the **Cabbages & Frocks** market (www.cabbagesandfrocks.co.uk) fills the garden of St Marylebone church with stalls selling vintage clothes and hot food.

The latest retail destination is Chiltern Street (pictured top right), a handsome Victorian-Gothic thoroughfare lined with some seriously swanky independent boutiques and cafés, located a few blocks west of the High Street. Fashionista faves include **Trunk** (no.8, W1U 7PU, 7486 2357, www.trunkclothiers.com) for dapper men's apparel; concept store **Mouki Mou** (no.29, W1U 7PL, 7224 4010, www.moukimou.com) for its delicately feminine (and pricey) clothes, jewellery and beauty items; and super-cool beachwear and sunglasses store **Prism** (no.54, W1U 7QX, 7935 5407, www.prismlondon.com).
www.marylebonevillage.com, www.chilternstreetw1.co.uk.

20 | Take afternoon tea

Afternoon tea has long been an institution at the **Ritz** (150 Piccadilly, W1J 9BR, 7493 8181, www.theritzlondon.com), but a new generation of establishments is challenging its teatime supremacy – not least the nearby **Wolseley** (160 Piccadilly, W1J 9EB, 7499 6996, www.thewolseley.com). An art deco beauty, it serves lavish stacks of finger sandwiches, scones and cakes; crisp linen, silver teapots and the odd celebrity sighting add to the sense of occasion.

The **Lobby Lounge** of the Corinthia Hotel (Whitehall Place, SW1A 2BD, 7930 8181, www.corinthia.com), off Trafalgar Square, is the sumptuous and serene setting for cake perfection. Come Christmas, the menu takes on a festive twist with offerings such as Santa's Little Helper (a chestnut -ream and blackcurrant macaroon topped with a sugar snowflake).

For a tea with a modern twist, try **Espelette** (Carlos Place, W1K 2AL, 3147 7100, www.the-connaught.co.uk), where the spread is as pretty as the Connaught hotel surrounds. Subtle updates on the classics are its forte, so wasabi-spiked salmon sandwiches or poppy and strawberry choux might appear alongside cucumber sarnies and chocolate cake. For a blend of old and new – and 17 blends of tea – there's the **English Tea Room** at Brown's Hotel (33 Albemarle Street, W1S 4BP, 7493 6020, www.brownshotel.com), which even offers a healthy 'Tea-Tox' version.

Fans of haute couture are advised to take tea in the **Caramel Room** at the Berkeley (Wilton Place, SW1X 7RL, 7235 6000, www.the-berkeley.co.uk), in Knightsbridge. Its 'Prêt-à-Portea' (pictured) changes every six months in line with the latest collections from the likes of Christopher Kane and Erdem: you might find yourself biting into a tiny handbag fashioned from orange sponge, or a fabulous polka-dot mini-dress made with chocolate and caramel crémeux. Wherever you choose, do book well in advance as the ritual of afternoon tea remains exceedingly popular.

21 Whitechapel Gallery

Founded in 1901, this East End gallery has always championed new talent, from Pablo Picasso (*Guernica* was exhibited here in 1939, its first and only visit to Britain) to Jackson Pollock and Gilbert & George. It still sets its own agenda, with rolling exhibitions that are sometimes offbeat, sometimes risqué, and almost always worth a closer look. Some inspired special events are held here too: an interview with fashion designer Giles Deacon, say, or a free children's illustration workshop led by conceptual artist Jake Chapman. An annual highlight is the London Open in summer, the Whitechapel's open-submission exhibition, first held in 1932.

77-82 Whitechapel High Street, E1 7QX (7522 7888, www.whitechapelgallery.org). Aldgate East tube.

22 Hampstead Heath

With its wide open vistas, tangled woodland and undulating hills, the Heath provides a welcome escape from the city. Picnickers sprawl in the overgrown meadows, dogs bound through the tall grasses with unbridled joy, and exotic-looking fungi lurk amid the trees; happily, the Heath's 800-odd acres are big enough to accommodate all-comers.

Taking a dip in the bathing ponds (Men's, Ladies' or Mixed) is a timeless London experience; while some hardy locals swim year-round, newcomers will find the water bracing, even at the height of summer.

North-west of the ponds, stately **Kenwood House** (0870 333 1181, www.english-heritage.org.uk) has recently undergone a grand refurbishment. It houses a fine collection of paintings and has a buzzing self-service café with a sheltered, sun-trap terrace.

Towards the southern edge of the Heath, Parliament Hill offers an extraordinary vista of the city skyline. Its slopes are generally dotted with kite-flyers – and if snow settles in the winter, half of north London turns up to risk life and limb on precarious makeshift sledges. From here, it's an enjoyable stroll into hilly little Hampstead village, with its genteel shops, cafés and restaurants, narrow streets and lovely pubs, including the **Holly Bush** (see no.44).

23 | Monument

Designed by Sir Christopher Wren and Robert Hooke as a memorial to the Great Fire of London, the Monument is the world's tallest freestanding stone column. It's an epic 311-step climb up the spiral staircase to the viewing platform: those who make it to the top are rewarded with dizzying views across London, and a certificate. From the ground to the gilded orb that crowns it, the Monument measures 202 feet – the precise distance from its base to Pudding Lane, where the blaze is thought to have started in a bakery on 2 September 1666.
Monument Street, EC3 (7626 2717, www.themonument.info). Monument tube.

24 The Shard

Designed by superstar architect Renzo Piano, this slender glass pyramid is visible from pretty much everywhere in the city – not surprising, really, considering it's the tallest building (at 1,016 feet) in London, and one of the tallest in the whole of Europe. High-speed lifts whisk visitors to stunning 360°, 40-mile views from the observation decks on floors 68, 69 and 72 – though it's just as fascinating looking down on the rooftops as out. For a more leisurely (and more expensive) way to admire the view, book into one of the tower's bars and restaurants, or even its luxury hotel.

32 London Bridge Street, SE1 9SG
(0844 499 7111, www.the-shard.com).
London Bridge tube/rail.

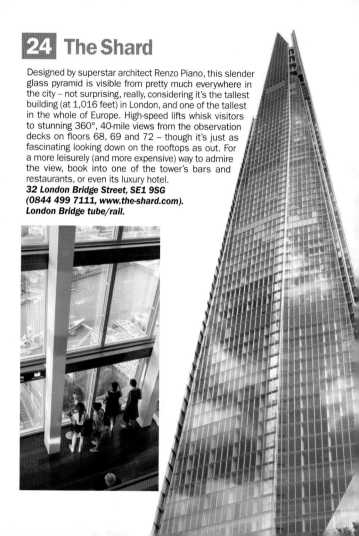

25 Chinatown

Just north of Leicester Square, a little pocket of central London has been the focus of London's Chinese community since the 1950s (www.chinatownlondon.org). Pagoda-topped phone boxes, Chinese bakeries selling sticky sweets and well-stocked grocery shops give pedestrianised Gerrard Street and the surrounding alleys an exotic feel, and there are a bewildering number of options if you fancy a meal.

Though the interiors aren't as smart as they once were, there's still a magical quality to the entrance of **Imperial China** (White Bear Yard, 25A Lisle Street, WC2H 7BA, 7734 3388, www.imperialchina-london.com), with its fishpond and dinky wooden footbridge; at the opposite end of the spectrum, **Jen Café** (4-8 Newport Place, WC2H 7JP, no phone) is as basic as it gets, but the noodles and dumplings – made by a lady sat right in the window – are excellent. If you've never experienced a hectic, Hong Kong-style dim sum trolley service, then a trip to the **New World Restaurant** (1 Gerrard Place, W1D 5PA, 7434 2508) will keep you on your toes. Or, if it's high-quality steamed dumplings you're after, including the best selection of *xiao long bau* (soup dumplings) in Chinatown, then head to **Dumplings' Legend** (15-16 Gerrard Street, W1D 6JE, 7494 1200, www.dumplingslegend.com). There's always decent roast duck to be had at **Four Seasons** (12 Gerrard Street, W1D 5PR, 7494 0870, www.fs-restaurants.co.uk). And if you're out in the small hours, you'll find sustenance – if not sophistication – at late-night spot **HK Diner** (22 Wardour Street, W1D 6QQ, 7434 9544, www.hkdiner.com).

But Chinatown is no longer about just Cantonese cooking, and hasn't been for some time. There's affordable Taiwanese food at **Old Tree Daiwan Bee** (26 Rupert Street, W1D 6DH, 8458 4112) and, if you're looking to get some fire in your belly, try some Sichuan street food – such as *dan dan* noodles, cucumber salad and crescent dumplings – at trendy pitstop **Baozi Inn** (25 Newport Court, WC2H 7JS, 7287 6877).

To see Chinatown at its most colourful, visit during Chinese New Year in late January or February: scarlet and gold dragons dance through the streets, drums and cymbals noisily ward off evil spirits, and firecrackers pop on the pavement.

DIM SUM ALL DAY

蛋黃酥
SESAME & SALTED EGG
PASTRY
£2.00

歡迎外

TAKEAWAY DELIV...
AVAILABLE

Following the river from its source in the Cotswolds, the Thames Path National Trail weaves through central London, hopping from bank to bank. It takes in all kinds of landscapes, from the glorious leafy surrounds of Richmond and Kew to the mini-Manhattan of skyscrapers on the Isle of Dogs. There's even a Victorian foot tunnel under the river, between the Isle of Dogs and Greenwich. Good public transport connections and riverboat services make it easy to tackle the walk in sections; for route details, see www.tfl.gov.uk/modes/walking/thames-path.

For sightseeing and people-watching, you can't beat the stretch along the South Bank from Westminster Bridge to Tower Bridge. It's crammed with London landmarks and cultural big-hitters, from the **London Eye** (no.49) to **Tate Modern** (no.75), and has fine views across the water to **Big Ben** (no.80), **St Paul's Cathedral** (no.45) and the **Tower of London** (no.2). This is also a lively slice of London life. Below the concrete bulk of the **Southbank Centre** (no.66), skateboarders perfect their kickflips and occasionally come a cropper, while arm-in-arm couples stroll along the

promenade or sip wine at the café-bar in front of **BFI Southbank** (no.18). The bookstalls here are always worth a browse too. In summer, look out for outdoor performances beside the recently revamped **National Theatre** (no.36). Buskers strum guitars, joggers puff past and, by the iconic Oxo Tower, artistic types build sand sculptures on the Thames 'beach'.

As dusk falls, the big sights are illuminated and the lights strung along the riverbanks are reflected in the water: for one of the loveliest views of the city by night, head to Waterloo Bridge.

27 Somerset House

Sandwiched between the grimy, traffic-choked Strand and the River Thames is a broad and calm neoclassical courtyard, with choreographed fountains that children can play in all day long if the weather's hot and their parents allow. Effectively a palatial 18th-century office block, Somerset House has a range of cafés and restaurants (some quite upmarket) and the Embankment Galleries, but really comes into its own with a regular programme of seasonal events. For winter, there's the ever-popular outdoor ice rink; in summer, open-air pop and rock concerts and alfresco film screenings take over the courtyard. It's also a key venue for London Fashion Week.

During the day, check out the amazing art in the **Courtauld Gallery** (7848 2526, www.courtauld.ac.uk/gallery). Although there are some outstanding early artworks (Cranach's wonderful *Adam & Eve*, for one), the collection's strongest suit is in Impressionist and post-Impressionist paintings: Manet's *A Bar at the Folies-Bergère*, alongside works by Monet, Cézanne, Gauguin and Van Gogh.

Strand, WC2R 1LA (7845 4600, www.somersethouse.org.uk).
Temple tube or Charing Cross tube/rail.

Short of a brisk walk, a 'Boris Bike' is the cheapest way to get around central London. The chunky blue and silver cycles – named by locals after Mayor Boris Johnson, who set up the scheme – are picked up from and returned to any of 700 self-service 'docking stations'. Launched in summer 2010, the scheme has since expanded far and wide: there are now 10,000 bikes to hire across the city. It's geared towards short hops rather than longer loans – journeys under 30 minutes are free, once you've paid £2 for 24 hours' access.

The bikes feature a bell, pedal-powered lights and a rack with an elastic cord with which to secure your possessions – though if you want to wear a cycle helmet, you'll need to bring your own.

If you're a regular rider, it makes sense to register for your own 'key' by signing up on the Transport for London website. More casual users gain temporary access by using the credit-card readers at docking stations. For more information on the scheme, visit www.tfl.gov.uk.

29 | Topshop

Over 250,000 shoppers enter the hallowed portals of Topshop's huge flagship store every week. Canny collaborations with famous designers (fashionista favourite Christopher Kane), supermodels (style icon Kate Moss) and hotly tipped young graduates have rocketed it to the front of the fashion pack, and into the wardrobe of many a bargain-loving celebrity. Unique, Topshop's premium line, now has its own adjoining store, with a separate entrance on Regent Street.

214 Oxford Street, W1W 8LG (0844 848 7487, www.topshop.com). Oxford Circus tube.

30 Royal Albert Hall & the Proms

Resplendent in red brick, this vast Victorian concert venue is a superb setting for the annual BBC Sir Henry Wood Promenade Concerts, better known as the Proms (0845 401 5040, www.bbc.co.uk/proms). Held between mid July and mid September, the Proms include around 70 concerts, running from early music recitals to orchestral world premières. You can book ahead, but £5 'promenade' tickets are available if you queue on the day, giving access to the standing-room stalls or the gallery at the very top of the auditorium. For the rest of the year, the programme mixes classical concerts with rock and pop acts, with spectacular choral performances and carol singalongs at Christmas.

Kensington Gore, SW7 2AP (0845 401 5045, www.royalalberthall. com). South Kensington tube or bus 9, 10, 52, 452.

The restaurant that jump-started the trend for Modern British food was **St John** (26 St John Street, EC1M 4AY, 7251 0848, www.stjohngroup. uk.com). Set near Smithfield meat market, it is famed for owner/chef Fergus Henderson's 'nose to tail' eating ethos, with offal, bone marrow and unfamiliar bits of beast often featuring on the menu. Lambs' tongues and tripe aren't for everyone, though, so the seasonally focused menu also caters to more squeamish souls with the likes of brill with fennel and green sauce, creamy cauliflower soup and good old-fashioned desserts: bread pudding with butterscotch sauce, for instance, or plum pie. Not to mention the legendary eccles cakes.

In the heart of the West End is Soho's **Hix** (66-70 Brewer Street, W1F 9UP, 7292 3518, www.hixsoho.co.uk; pictured above), a showcase for Mark Hix's considerable culinary talents. Native oysters, roast grouse and hanger steak are regulars on the menu. Before dinner, head down to the basement for a precision-mixed cocktail in Mark's Bar.

Just round the corner is **Social Eating House** (58-59 Poland Street, W1F 7NR, 7993 3251, www.socialeatinghouse.com; pictured below), another corker of a restaurant from chef-patron Jason Atherton, current star of London's dining scene. From Kentish salt-marsh lamb to Cornish sea bass, smoked Shetland salmon to Lincolnshire Poacher cheese, provenance is key here. Expect supercharged flavours and immaculate presentation. The Blind Pig cocktail bar on the top floor is a winner too.

Superb British produce, cooked with a minimum of fuss, is the mainstay at busy little **Hereford Road** (3 Hereford Road, W2 4AB, 7727 1144, www.herefordroad.org) in Bayswater. Dishes such as potted crab or partridge with lentils and girolles are as simple as they are satisfying. Save room for the magnificent desserts.

With its white wood cladding, tractor decor and rustic furniture, the **Shed** (122 Palace Gardens Terrace, W8 4RT, 7229 4024, www.theshed-restaurant.com) in Notting Hill certainly looks the part. The small-plates menu is inventive without being tricksy, and many ingredients come from the owners' family farm in Nutbourne, West Sussex, as does the wine.

▶ *London's laid-back gastropubs also offer some fine Modern British cooking; see no.85.*

Egyptian sarcophagus, carved from a single piece of alabaster.

Here too is the parlour Soane designed for Padre Giovanni, an entirely imaginary medieval monk; the good Padre's 'tomb' – which, in fact, houses the remains of Soane's lap dog, Fanny – is out in the courtyard.

The candlelit tours held on the first Tuesday of the month are a brilliantly atmospheric way to appreciate the museum, though be prepared to queue. **13 Lincoln's Inn Fields, WC2A 3BP (7405 2107, www.soane. org). Holborn tube.**

No.13 Lincoln's Inn Fields was home to Georgian architect Sir John Soane – and having become a museum after his death in 1837, its wonderful eccentricity remains perfectly preserved. A quite extraordinary array of art and antiquities fills every nook and cranny of the labyrinthine interior, taking in Grecian sculptures, crumbling architectural fragments and assorted busts, bronzes and curiosities. The Picture Room is crammed with treasures, some of which are hidden away in ingenious fold-out panels; in pride of place is Hogarth's *A Rake's Progress*, whose eight paintings chart the downfall of a spendthrift young dandy. Downstairs are the death masks and the stately funerary urns of the Crypt, whose centrepiece is a huge

33 Museum of London

To explore the history of London from before the Romans arrived to the present, there's no better place than the superb Museum of London.

Head to the lower ground floor to learn about the modern metropolis, starting with the Great Fire in 1666. Highlights include a recreated Georgian pleasure garden, whose mannequins sport historic dresses matched with contemporary Philip Treacy masks and hats; an actual 18th-century debtor's prison cell, with graffiti still clearly legible; and the Lord Mayor's dazzling gold coach, which is wheeled out of the gallery each November for a starring role in the Lord Mayor's Show (see no.39). By far the most moving exhibit, though, is the Blitz gallery. Beneath an unexploded World War II bomb, starkly suspended from the ceiling in a glass case, runs the heart-rending but often surprisingly good-humoured testimony of ordinary survivors of the German bombs, bringing Londoners' famous 'Blitz spirit' to life.

Upstairs is where to see Roman and medieval remains, including some sharply pointed shoes – the height of fashion in the 1380s, apparently – and the death mask of Oliver Cromwell.

150 London Wall, EC2Y 5HN (7001 9844, www.museum oflondon.org.uk). Barbican or St Paul's tube.

34 | Dulwich Picture Gallery

This diminutive gallery makes for a fine afternoon's excursion, punching well above its weight with its collection of Old Masters. Works by Rembrandt, Rubens and Gainsborough are among those showcased in the quietly dignified neoclassical premises, built in 1811 by Sir John Soane. After admiring the paintings, check out the curious lighting effects in the mausoleum (built by Soane for the gallery's founders), then stop for lunch in the elegant, airy little café or have a picnic on the lawn. *Gallery Road, SE21 7AD (8693 5254, www.dulwichpicturegallery. org.uk). North Dulwich or West Dulwich rail.*

Atmosphere is everything at this little museum. Up a steep spiral staircase are cases of brutal old surgical tools, bunches of herbs and unmentionable things in jars. The star of the show, however, is a pre-anaesthetic operating theatre with tiered viewing seats for students, which dates from 1822. Book ahead for one of the brilliantly convincing surgical re-enactments – if you've got a strong stomach.
9A St Thomas's Street, SE1 9RY (7188 2679, www.thegarret.org.uk). London Bridge tube/rail.

36 | National Theatre

As you'd expect, the NT stages plenty of serious productions in its three auditoriums, featuring a stellar cast of actors and directors. Shakespearean tragedies share the bill with revivals of long-neglected classics and all manner of new productions, from smaller-scale experimental pieces to the big-budget likes of *War Horse*. Yet despite its impeccable artistic credentials, the National is far from staid, with free early-evening concerts in the foyer taking in everything from foot-stamping flamenco to boogie-woogie piano, and some brilliant kids' craft and theatre skills workshops. Look out for Travelex-sponsored performances, when many tickets cost just £15, and the free outdoor Watch This Space Festival in summer. Changes are underway too, with the arrival of new artistic director Rufus Norris and a revamp of the building (a classic of 1970s concrete brutalism, hated and loved in equal measure) that's resulted in a brand-new bookshop, bar, café and entrance.

South Bank, SE1 9PX (7452 3400, www.nationaltheatre.org.uk).
Embankment or Southwark tube, or Waterloo tube/rail.

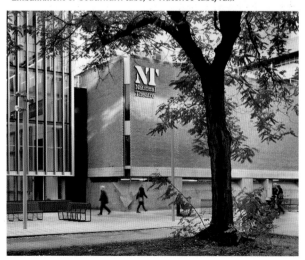

37 | Camden Market

Counterculture and commerce meet at Camden Market, which is at its chaotic best at the weekend. Trousers bristling with spikes, neon tutus and army fatigues are among the goods, along with battered cowboy boots, swirly 1970s frocks and arty-crafty accessories. You'll see more mohicans here than anywhere else in London, while lashings of black eyeliner are an essential for the teenagers who loiter beside Camden Lock. The market's various subsections sprawl north from Camden Town tube, with tentacles reaching out alongside the canal, up Inverness Street, around Camden Lock (head to the West Yard for the best food stalls), into Stables Market (known for its vintage dealers) and the Horse Hospital. On Sunday afternoons, Camden Town tube is exit-only: catch a bus or walk north beyond the market to Chalk Farm station.

38 | Kensington Palace

Kensington Palace packs a lot of history into a relatively small red-brick building. Built in 1605, the original merchant's house was expanded by Sir Christopher Wren after William III and Mary II bought the place in 1689; the asthmatic king found the air more congenial than on damp, polluted Whitehall. Queen Victoria was born in the palace in 1819, and it was here, in 1837, that the formerly carefree young princess learnt that the death of her uncle, William IV, had made her queen. More recently, in 1997, the funeral procession for Diana, Princess of Wales, set off from Kensington Palace. It's still a royal home: the Duke and Duchess of Cambridge have lived here since 2013.

Both the building and grounds have been reinvigorated by a recent £12 million revamp. The Queen's and King's State Apartments are as splendid as you'd hope, while the Fashion Rules exhibition (until summer 2015) displays some fabulous frocks belonging to a trio of extremely well dressed royal women: the Queen; her sister, Princess Margaret; and Lady Di. If you fancy taking afternoon tea during your visit, the formal Sunken Garden is a beautiful setting for the opulent Orangery café.

Kensington Gardens, W8 4PX (0844 482 7777, www.hrp.org.uk).
High Street Kensington or Queensway tube.

39 Fireworks

Londoners have always loved fireworks – after all, as far back as 1749 Handel composed music to accompany a display in Green Park. Nowadays, some of the most spectacular displays explode over the Thames, with the city's cluster of central bridges providing superb vantage points.

Autumn is the peak season: the **Totally Thames Festival** (7928 8998, www.totallythames.org) during September and the **Lord Mayor's Show** (7332 3456, www.lordmayorsshow.london) in early November both usually close with an impressive bang, while the handy confluence of Diwali (the Hindu Festival of Light) and Bonfire Night (the traditional commemoration of Guy Fawkes' 1605 failure to blow up the Houses of Parliament) makes the weekend nearest to the **Fifth of November** a feast of fiery fun. Battersea Park, Brockwell Park, Ravenscourt Park, Alexandra Palace and Blackheath usually have enormous bonfires and spectacular fireworks, but you could also pre-book a late ride on the **London Eye** (see no.49) to see displays all over town.

The city's official **New Year's Eve Fireworks**, at the Southbank, are always fantastic – but you need a ticket (on sale from September) to get into the viewing areas.

40 Barbican Centre

Walkways lead past the Barbican Estate's rectangular ponds and artistically angular towers of flats to reach Europe's largest multi-arts centre, set by a central lakeside terrace. Its programming is brilliantly varied, taking in gigs by cult rock stars, concerts from the resident London Symphony Orchestra, flying visits from international dance companies and inspired film screenings, from classic Hitchcock to Japanese horror. Exhibitions are equally bold, with a heady blend of architecture, fashion, art and design, and there are regular tours of the estate itself – a landmark of Modernist architecture.

Silk Street, EC2Y 8DS (7638 4141, www.barbican.org.uk).
Barbican tube or Moorgate tube/rail.

41 | Fortnum & Mason

This plush temple to fine foods, teas and wines is in good fettle after more than 300 years in business. Its premises on Piccadilly ooze understated luxury: even the rooftop beehives, which supply the store's own-brand honey, are palatial affairs, painted in Fortnum's signature shade of blue-green eau-de-nil. Goods range from truffles to terrines (not forgetting the famous hampers), and there are five impressive restaurants; in the plush 1707 wine bar, you can sip a bottle of your choice from the excellent wine department on payment of a £10 corkage fee.

181 Piccadilly, W1A 1ER (7734 8040, www.fortnumandmason. co.uk). Green Park or Piccadilly Circus tube.

42 | The O2

Standing in splendour on the tip of the Greenwich peninsula, the dome of this huge arena, with its 12 yellow masts, has become a modern London landmark. Originally built to mark the millennium, the vast space has been reinvented as a multi-talented venue – host to spectacular pop and rock gigs and blockbuster sporting events. Towering talents from the NBA, beefy WWE wrestlers, Olympic gymnasts and top-seeded tennis players have all battled it out in front of the crowds here. The complex also takes in the smaller Indigo venue plus Building Six for club nights; Brooklyn Bowl's ten-pin bowling alley and gig space; a multiplex that includes one super-sized cinema screen; and numerous restaurants and cafés. You can even book 'Up at the O2' tickets (www.theo2.co.uk/upattheo2) to walk right over the top of the dome, safely attached to a security line. *Millennium Way, SE10 0BB (8463 2000 information, 0844 856 0202 tickets, www.theo2.co.uk). North Greenwich tube.*

▶ *The most scenic way to get to and from the arena is by river, aboard a Thames Clipper; see no.15.*

43 | Wallace Collection

Discreetly located on a quiet Marylebone square, the Wallace is a delight. The galleries contain an unusual combination of arms and armour, furniture, porcelain and glassware, sculpture and exquisite objets d'art, but the real thrill is seeing artistic masterpieces in a relaxed townhouse setting. 'Masterpieces' is no exaggeration: paintings by Gainsborough, Poussin, Rembrandt, Titian and Velázquez are on display, as is Frans Hals' *Laughing Cavalier*. And now they're looking better than ever, after a recent revamp of the Great Gallery (pictured). Admission is free.
Hertford House, Manchester Square, W1U 3BN (7563 9500, www. wallacecollection.org). Bond Street tube.

44 | Have a pint

Gastropubs and slick cocktail bars are all very well, but sometimes all you want is a decent pint in a friendly, old-fashioned boozer. For sheer Victorian splendour, the **Princess Louise** (208-209 High Holborn, WC1V 7EP, 7405 8816, www.princesslouisepub.co.uk; pictured top left, top right & bottom right) in Holborn is unrivalled. Its darkly cosy, wood-panelled interior, stucco ceiling and intricate etched glass are wonderfully grand – but as it's a Samuel Smith's pub, beer is refreshingly cheap. A 15-minute walk away, just off Hatton Garden, the tiny, oak-fronted **Ye Olde Mitre** (1 Ely Court, Ely Place, EC1N 6SJ, 7405 4751, www.yeoldemitreholborn. co.uk) offers a more intimate drinking experience. Notoriously tricky to find, it's open weekdays only; those that do stumble upon it are rewarded by well-kept real ales and delightfully crooked, cramped surrounds.

Another diminutive gem is the **Lamb & Flag** (33 Rose Street, WC2E 9EB, 7497 9504, www.lambandflagcoventgarden.co.uk), squirrelled away down an alley in the heart of Covent Garden. Two centuries' worth of cuttings and caricatures adorn the walls, while the classic pub grub on offer includes cod and chips, and steak and ale pie; come in the afternoon to avoid the after-work rush. Crowds spill into the streets on summer evenings, while the fire emits a hospitable glow on chilly winter days. Up in Hampstead, the **Holly Bush** (22 Holly Mount, NW3 6SG, 7435 2892, www.hollybushhampstead.co.uk; pictured bottom left) is another old-fashioned boozer with a welcoming fire in the grate. It's a low-ceilinged, inviting place with cask ales and battered oak settles – ideal after a walk across the Heath.

In summer, the great British beer garden comes into its own – and one of the nicest spots for an alfresco pint is the tranquil walled terrace at the **Albion** (10 Thornhill Road, N1 1HW, 7607 7450, www.the-albion.co.uk), a polished-up Georgian beauty in Islington that's known for its superior Sunday roasts. Its wisteria-entwined pergola, wooden tables and herb garden ooze rustic charm.

If you'd prefer a view over the Thames, follow in the footsteps of Graham Greene, Dylan Thomas and Ernest Hemingway and head for the **Dove** (19 Upper Mall, W6 9TA, 8748 9474, www.dovehammersmith.co.uk) in Hammersmith. The 17th-century beamed interior is full of character, but on sunny days the best seats in the house are on the little Thames-side terrace.

45 St Paul's Cathedral

Over the last decade, a £40m restoration project has removed much of the Victorian grime from Sir Christopher Wren's cathedral, and the façade looks as bright as it must have done when the last stone was placed in 1708. Up in the Whispering Gallery, the acoustics are so good that a whisper can carry to the opposite side of the dome; keep on climbing to the exterior Golden Gallery for spectacular City views. If the steps are too much, head down into the maze-like crypt; here, in addition to Nelson's grand tomb and Wren's small, plain memorial, you'll find a 270° film that recounts the cathedral's history and flies you to the top of the dome.
Ludgate Hill, EC4M 8AD (7246 8357, www.stpauls.co.uk).
St Paul's tube.

46 | Science Museum

The sheer scale of the Science Museum impresses. Straight after the bag check, you're confronted by enormous 18th-century steam engines in the Energy Hall, while rockets are suspended from the ceiling in the Exploring Space gallery. Alongside the *Apollo 10* capsule, displays explain how astronauts eat, sleep and go to the loo in space. There are more iconic objects in Making the Modern World, ranging from Stephenson's *Rocket* locomotive to a chunky 1980s mobile phone.

Five further floors explore computing, flight, mathematics, medicine and astronomy, with child-friendly pulleys, explosions and other interactive experiments in the third-floor Launchpad gallery. Don't miss the futuristic-looking silver pods in Who Am I? Here, you can find out what gender your brain is, see what you'll look like in ten years' time, and discover what makes you unique – if you can get past the crowds of eager children, that is. The newest (and biggest) gallery is Information Age, which looks at communication technologies over the past 200 years, from the development of the telegraph to the sophisticated microprocessors of today.

Admission to the permanent collections is free, though some of the more exotic interactives – the Legend of Apollo 4D space trip, the Fly Zone flight simulation, films in the IMAX cinema – cost extra.

Exhibition Road, SW7 2DD (7942 4000 switchboard, 0870 870 4868 information, www.sciencemuseum.org.uk). South Kensington tube.

▶ *South Kensington's trio of Victorian museums also includes the V&A (see no.3) and the Natural History Museum (see no.83).*

Lying the shadows of the City's skyscrapers, the area around Spitalfields and Brick Lane is perfect for a leisurely Sunday browse, with offbeat shops, market stalls, street eats and cafés.

The days of wholesale fruit and veg are long gone at the Victorian **Old Spitalfields Market** (7247 8556, www.oldspitalfieldsmarket.com; pictured). Instead, expect an arty array of hand-printed T-shirts, vintage frocks, bric-a-brac and food stalls, surrounded by a sleek shopping precinct. The main market days are from Thursday (when there's a good antiques market) to Sunday (the busiest and best). Come with spending money, as cashpoints are in short supply.

Next, press on to the **Sunday Upmarket** (7770 6028, www.sunday upmarket.co.uk), in the nearby Truman Brewery, which has a crafty fashion vibe all of its own. Homespun food stalls sell everything from thalis to tapas, and there are plenty of unusual clothes, gifts and accessories being sold by fresh-faced young designers.

Truman Brewery yard opens on to **Brick Lane** (www.visitbricklane.org), lined with Bangladeshi cafés, curry houses and sari shops to the south, as well as quirky boutiques and vintage specialists to the north. Don't miss the side roads off Brick Lane, which hold the likes of **Vintage Emporium** (14 Bacon Street, E1 6LF, 7739 0799) and **Absolute Vintage** (15 Hanbury Street, E1 6QR, 7247 3883, www.absolutevintage.co.uk), and make sure you get a bagel or two from **Brick Lane Beigel Bake** (159 Brick Lane, E1 6SB, 7729 0616).

Off the top of Brick Lane is **Redchurch Street**, now a destination in its own right thanks to the likes of some ultra-hip fashion shops (APC, Hostem, Sunspel) alongside retro household goods at **Labour & Wait** (85 Redchurch Street, E2 7DJ, 7729 6253, www.labourandwait.co.uk). Meanwhile, mainstream brands and indies populate the black-painted shipping containers that make up nearby **Boxpark** (www.boxpark.co.uk), on the corner of Bethnal Green Road.

48 WWT London Wetland Centre

A mere four miles from central London, this 104-acre nature reserve feels half a world away. The tranquil ponds, rustling reedbeds and wildflower meadows teem with bird life – some 200 species have been spotted here – and are home to the now-rare water vole and a family of Asian short-clawed otters. Regular events include daily guided tours and feeding sessions, and bat walks in August and September.

Queen Elizabeth's Walk, SW13 9WT (8409 4400, www.wwt.org.uk/wetland-centres/london). Hammersmith tube then bus 283, or Barnes rail, or bus 33, 72, 209.

49 | London Eye

For unrivalled views across the city, head 443 feet skywards in one of the London Eye's glass pods. The pods take half an hour to travel the 1,392-foot circumference of the wheel, and from the top – if you're lucky and the weather's clear – you can see as far as Windsor Castle, some 25 miles away.

Jubilee Gardens, SE1 7PB (0871 781 3000, www.londoneye.com). Westminster tube or Waterloo tube/rail.

50 | Tower Bridge

So distinctive that Nazi bombers used it as a navigation aid during the Blitz, Tower Bridge (built 1886-94) has a drawbridge design that allows big ships to pass through. It still regularly raises its double bascules (now powered by electricity rather than steam), sometimes several times a day. To see it in action, consult the website for scheduled times, or follow the Twitter updates (www.twitter.com/towerbridge). Visit the exhibition and you can take in the view from the high-level walkway (a spectacular glass floor was added in 2014) that connects the two spiky towers, and explore the engine rooms.

Tower Bridge Exhibition, Tower Bridge, SE1 2UP (7403 3761, www.towerbridge.org.uk). Tower Hill tube or Tower Gateway DLR.

51 Museum of London Docklands

A lofty Georgian warehouse accommodates this huge museum, which explores the history of London's docklands and the River Thames. In the Sailortown gallery, you can wander a re-creation of the narrow streets of Wapping as they were some 150 years ago, complete with the sound of drunken sailors and a wild animal emporium. Other exhibitions carry a real emotional charge – not least the London, Sugar & Slavery exhibition, which explores the city's involvement in the transatlantic slave trade. *No.1 Warehouse, West India Quay, Hertsmere Road, E14 4AL (7001 9844, www.museumoflondon.org.uk/docklands). Canary Wharf tube or West India Quay DLR.*

52 | HMS Belfast

Now a floating outpost of the Imperial War Museum, this 11,500-tonne battlecruiser is the last surviving big-gun World War II warship in Europe, and played a key role in the D-Day landings. Excited children dart up the steep, narrow ladders and tear around her gun turrets, bridge, decks and engine room, while a free audio guide reveals what life was like on board (decidedly cramped, with up to 950 sailors in residence).

The Queen's Walk, SE1 2JH (7940 6300, www.iwm.org.uk/ visits/hms-belfast). London Bridge tube/rail.

53 Hyde Park & Kensington Gardens

Occupying a 350-acre slice of central London, Hyde Park (www.royalparks.org.uk) has a long and varied history. In the 18th century, the smart set trotted along Rotten Row on horseback; in June 1908, 250,000 suffragettes shocked polite society when they gathered here to demand votes for women. Marches and protests still take place in the park, and on Sunday mornings all sorts of people clamber on to boxes to exercise their freedom of speech at Speakers' Corner, as they have done since 1872; some are less than coherent, but the heckling and banter is always entertaining.

The lower end of the park is given over to the waterfowl and boats of the Serpentine, with little pedalos and rowing boats for hire from Easter to October. Test the water temperature by swimming in the roped-off lido, alongside the ducks. To the south of the Serpentine, by the lido, the Diana, Princess of Wales, Memorial Fountain is a calming, gently curving channel made from smooth Cornish granite.

To the west, lovely Kensington Gardens takes in stately Italian gardens, avenues of trees and the famous bronze statue of Peter Pan beside the Long Water. The superb Diana Memorial Playground is also Peter Pan-themed, with a resplendent wooden pirate ship at its centre. Art lovers will enjoy the small but inventive **Serpentine Gallery** (7402 6075, www.serpentinegalleries.org), which hosts modern and contemporary art exhibitions. Nearby, its new offshoot, the Zaha Hadid-designed **Serpentine Sackler Gallery**, provides a handsome cultural destination in what was once a gunpowder depot. Afterwards, wander down to Sir George Gilbert Scott's extravagant Albert Memorial – Victorian pomp and splendour at its most gloriously overblown.

▶ *From the western end of Kensington Gardens, it's the shortest of strolls to Kensington Palace; see no.38.*

54 | Geffrye Museum

Peek into Londoners' living rooms at this delightful museum, a converted set of 18th-century almshouses. The 11 recreated rooms skip through the centuries, from 1600 to the present day, and there are temporary exhibitions; the rooms always get a charming Christmas-themed makeover from November to early January. The pleasure of exploring the Geffrye is in the details (a bell jar of stuffed birds, perhaps, or a 1960s bubble TV). There are evening events and daytime children's activities. Pretty period gardens (open April to October) are hidden at the rear. *136 Kingsland Road, E2 8EA (7739 9893, www.geffrye-museum. org.uk). Hoxton rail.*

55 | Westfield London

For retail therapy on a grand scale, head to this vast shopping mall in west London. With more than 300 shops, it has all the high-street names one could need, from Accessorize to Zara, while the presence of fashion big-hitters (in the upmarket Village section) including Louis Vuitton, Burberry and Prada adds a haute-couture edge to proceedings. A host of cafés and restaurants revive footsore shoppers, and solicitous concierges smooth the way to consumer nirvana with a raft of extra services – from valet parking to 'handsfree' shopping – some free, some not.

Over in east London is Westfield Stratford City, complete with bowling alley, casino and multiplex, not to mention a branch of John Lewis.
Ariel Way, W12 7GF (3371 2300, www.westfield.com/london).
White City or Wood Lane tube, or Shepherd's Bush tube/rail.

Although the seedy Soho of gangsters, pimps and strip clubs is nowadays mostly consigned to black and white photographs, this is still a lively area to visit. Much of the daytime action happens along or near Old Compton Street – a gay-friendly superhighway of streetside cafés – or else among the loungers and layabouts who populate the four teeny lawns of Soho Square (pictured below right) at the first hint of sunshine.

Berwick Street, with its second-hand vinyl shops, fabric specialists and high-design dim sum teahouse **Yauatcha** (15 Broadwick Street, W1F 0DL, 7494 8888, www.yauatcha.com), gives an appropriately jumbled flavour of modern Soho – though its rough-and-tumble fruit market is in danger of getting squeezed out of existence by new luxe apartments and general gentrification. With the sex trade retreating to a few dark corners (peep shows linger at Tisbury Court and the eastern end of Brewer Street), the prevailing Soho industries are media-related. West Soho has remodelled itself as a shopping destination, with Carnaby Street and the surrounding alleys home to the kind of chic fashion and beauty boutiques that were common in its swinging '60s heyday.

The need to feed the media crowd has resulted in some superb restaurants, including **Hix** and **Social Eating House** (for both, see no. 31), as well as a slew of new-wave cafés, such as **Milkbar** (3 Bateman Street, W1D 4AG, 7287 4796, www.milkbarsoho.co.uk) and Spanish-slanted mini-chain **Fernandez & Wells** (73 Beak Street, W1F 9SR, 7287 8124, and 43 Lexington Street, W1F 9AL, 7734 1546, www.fernandezandwells.com). Few of the Italian delis and cafés that once populated the neighbourhood remain – the open-all-hours 1950s caff **Bar Italia** (22 Frith Street, W1D 4RP, 7437 4520, www.baritaliasoho.co.uk) is a vibrant exception. Old Soho lives on too at the louche **French House** pub (49 Dean Street, W1D 5BG, 7437 2477, www.frenchhousesoho.com), traditional French pâtisserie **Maison Bertaux** (28 Greek Street, W1D 5DQ, 7437 6007, www.maisonbertaux.com; pictured top right) and legendary jazz club **Ronnie Scott's** (47 Frith Street, W1D 4HT, 7439 0747, www.ronniescotts.co.uk).

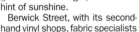

57 Royal Botanic Gardens (Kew Gardens)

Kew's 300 acres take in a spectacular array of plants, from carnivorous monsters on the lookout for passing insects to centuries-old oaks. There's nothing quite like wandering amid the verdant foliage and exotic blooms in the humid Palm House on a cold winter's day; come March, the gardens' carpet of purple and white crocuses is one of the first signs of spring. For a leafy, lofty perspective, stroll through the treetops on the Xstrata Treetop Walkway, some 60 feet above ground.

Kew, Surrey TW9 3AB (8332 5655, www.kew.org). Kew Gardens tube/rail, Kew Bridge rail or riverboat to Kew Pier.

58 National Gallery

The National Gallery contains a bewildering number of must-see paintings from the world's finest artists – Cézanne's *Bathers*, one of the *Sunflowers* paintings by Van Gogh, Constable's *The Hay Wain*, and *The Fighting Temeraire* by Turner among them. If you're not sure where to start, use the ArtStart touchscreens in the Sainsbury Wing or the East Wing Espresso Bar to choose a themed tour, or plot your own course through the highlights (you can print your route for free). Also in the Sainsbury Wing, there's great artistry in the cooking at the National Dining Rooms (the attached bakery-café is a cheaper option), while the East Wing contains the darkly handsome – and late-opening – National Café. *Trafalgar Square, WC2N 5DN (7747 2885, www.nationalgallery. org.uk). Leicester Square tube or Charing Cross tube/rail.*

65

The capital has its fair share of pricey fine-dining restaurants, but you don't have to spend a fortune to enjoy a taste of the high life.

The set lunch at **Pied à Terre** (34 Charlotte Street, W1T 2NH, 7636 1178, www.pied-a-terre. co.uk; pictured near right) is one of the best bargains in town, at £27.50 for two courses (canapés included). The dining room may be slightly austere, but Michelin-starred chef Marcus Eaves assembles his dishes with the eye of an artist, often including tiny edible flowers or herbs picked from the little rooftop garden.

In Soho, British-oriented **Quo Vadis** (26-29 Dean Street, W1D 3LL, 7437 9585, www.quovadissoho.co.uk; pictured top right) is a true rarity in offering a set menu not just at lunch but throughout the day. The Theatre Set costs £17.50 for two courses or £20 for three, with a choice of two dishes (including vegetarian options) at each stage.

The set lunch at **Little Social** (5 Pollen Street, W1S 1NE, 7870 3730, www.littlesocial.co.uk) costs £28 for two courses, £35 for three. This may not be London's cheapest, but it's certainly cheap for Mayfair – one of the most expensive areas of London. And it's the most wallet-friendly way to sample the cooking of chef-patron Jason Atherton, whose restaurants are among the best in town for modern-style French-inspired cooking.

Medlar (438 King's Road, SW10 0LJ, 7349 1900, www.medlar restaurant.co.uk), in Chelsea, is worth a special trip for some of the most imaginative and accomplished Modern European cooking in London. And the set lunch (Monday to Saturday) is a real bargain: £20/£25/£30 for one/two/three courses.

Most restaurants offer their set lunch on weekdays only. Long-established and much-loved seafood specialist **J Sheekey** (28-32 St Martin's Court, WC2N 4AL, 7240 2565, www.j-sheekey.co.uk, pictured bottom right) swims against the tide by going for Saturday and Sunday instead. It's a bargain at £26.50 for three courses, and the options include vegetarian and meat or game dishes as well as fish.

60 | Westminster Cathedral

The most important Catholic church in England is a somewhat surprising sight among the office blocks of Victoria. With its Byzantine domes, arches and soaring tower, it would look more at home in the middle of Istanbul. No wonder: architect John Francis Bentley, who built it between 1895 and 1903, was heavily influenced by the Hagia Sophia. The interior is richly adorned with mosaics and marble, while 'Treasures of the Cathedral' (admission charged) displays an impressive Arts and Crafts coronet, a Tudor chalice, holy relics and Bentley's amazing architectural model of his cathedral, complete with tiny hawks. A lift runs 210 feet up the bell tower for great views over this historic district.

42 Francis Street, SW1P 1QW (7798 9055, www.westminster cathedral.org.uk). Victoria tube/rail.

61 | Shakespeare's Globe

Experience theatre Elizabethan-style at this oak-beamed reconstruction of the Globe Theatre (the original, co-owned by William Shakespeare, burned to the ground in 1613). That means open-air performances and hard wooden benches; paying a little extra to rent a cushion is money well spent. It's standing-room only if you're a 'groundling' in the yard – a mere £5 a ticket, and thrillingly close to the onstage action. The new Sam Wanamaker Playhouse – an intimate indoor wooden theatre, lit only by candlelight – opened in 2014.

21 New Globe Walk, Bankside, SE1 9DT (7402 1400, www.shakespearesglobe.com). Southwark tube or London Bridge tube/rail.

62 | Ride the Routemaster

London's classic double-deckers were withdrawn from general service in 2005, but a few beautifully refurbished Routemasters still run on one central London route. The 15 bus departs from Cockspur Street, at the south-west corner of Trafalgar Square (Stop S), every 15 minutes from 9.30am to 6.30pm. It potters east through the City to the Tower of London, via St Paul's Cathedral. Regular tickets and Travelcards are valid, but you must buy them before boarding the bus.

Introduced in 2012, the New Routemaster bus is an increasingly common sight on the city's streets. It's a handsome vehicle with a classic hop-on, hop-off platform at the rear (not always in operation), but, bus aficionados insist, not a patch on the original design.

63 | City Farms

For a slice of country life in the midst of the city, check out one of London's many city farms. The biggest is **Mudchute Park & Farm** (Pier Street, Isle of Dogs, E14 3HP, 7515 5901, www.mudchute.org), where you can stand in a meadow full of grazing sheep while taking in the soaring skyscrapers of Canary Wharf. Mild-eyed cows, inquisitive llamas and sprightly Indian runner ducks are among the residents, along with cuddly beasties for children to pet; after meeting the animals, refuel at the Mudchute Kitchen. Another favourite is **Hackney City Farm** (1A Goldsmiths Row, E2 8QA, 7729 6381, www.hackneycityfarm.co.uk; pictured). In spring, you might meet a wobbly-legged newborn lamb, and there are always rabbits, chinchillas and guinea pigs to coo over. Stop for lunch at the Frizzante café, then head home with a box of freshly laid eggs. In south London, **Crystal Palace Park Farm** (Capel Manor College, Ledrington Road, SE19 2BS, 8659 2557, www.capel.ac.uk/crystal-palace-park-farm.html) has paddocks and a small yard, as well as lovely views. Along with the usual small furries, there are Shetland ponies, kunekune pigs and reptiles. The farm has no café, but the surrounding parkland is great for picnics.

For a full list of city farms, consult the **Federation of City Farms & Community Gardens** (0117 923 1800, www.farmgarden.org.uk).

The IWM's imposing premises were once a notorious lunatic asylum (the Bethlehem Royal Hospital, aka Bedlam). A £40 million revamp, completed in 2014, has resulted in a spectacular new central atrium, where a Harrier jet and a Spitfire are suspended above a German V1 flying bomb and a Reuters Land Rover damaged by a rocket attack in Gaza. The two world wars are covered in depth (the galleries devoted to World War I have been extended and redesigned), while the Holocaust Exhibition (not recommended for under-14s) traces the history of European anti-Semitism to its nadir in the concentration camps. Secret War examines espionage and counter-intelligence, with a child-friendly angle provided by the new interactive exhibition Horrible Histories: Spies.

Lambeth Road, SE1 6HZ (7416 5000, www.iwm.org.uk).
Lambeth North tube or Elephant & Castle tube/rail.

65 | Wembley Stadium

For football fans, the new Wembley Stadium is no less a shrine than its predecessor, no matter that the iconic twin towers have given way to architecture supremo Lord Foster's landmark leaning arch. Highlights of a tour include sitting in the manager's dug-out and the home dressing room, and climbing the Trophy Winners' steps to the Royal Box, where you get to lay a hand on a (very valuable) replica of the FA Cup. Wembley hosted the final of the Champions League, Europe's premier club football competition, in 2013.

Stadium Way, Wembley, Middx HA9 0WS (0844 980 8001, www. wembleystadium.com). Wembley Park tube or Wembley Stadium rail.

66 Southbank Centre

Opened in 1951 as the centrepiece of the Festival of Britain, the Royal Festival Hall was wonderfully refurbished a few years back. Now the bars and restaurants – many of which look out over the Thames – hum with life all day. Under artistic director Jude Kelly, the programming has really come to life too, mixing cult bands and fun musicals with string quartets and classical concerts, and children's events with author readings. Regular festivals include music-oriented Meltdown in June and a pre-Christmas extravaganza. Next door to the RFH, the Queen Elizabeth Hall and Purcell Room host recitals and smaller events, while the Hayward Gallery displays changing exhibitions of contemporary art.
South Bank, Belvedere Road, SE1 8XX (7960 4200, www.southbankcentre.co.uk). Embankment tube or Waterloo tube/rail.

67 Portobello Market

Famed for its antiques and collectibles, this is actually several markets rolled into one. The Saturday antiques market starts at the Notting Hill end; further up are food stalls and, under the Westway and along the walkway to Ladbroke Grove, emerging designers and vintage clothes dealers (Fridays and Saturdays, with Friday the less frantic of the two). Carry cash, as the cashpoint on the main drag is invariably mobbed.
Portobello Road, W10 (www.portobellomarket.org).
Ladbroke Grove or Notting Hill Gate tube.

68 Hampton Court Palace

Everyone seems to fall in love with this spectacular red-brick palace. It was built in 1514 by Cardinal Wolsey, but Henry VIII liked it so much that he seized it in 1528. Even dour Oliver Cromwell took a shine to the place, moving in after the Civil War. Elizabeth I was probably less keen: she was imprisoned here by her elder sister Mary.

Just strolling through the courtyards and corridors is a pleasure, but there are plenty of highlights. The Great Hall, part of Henry VIII's State Apartments, is famed for its beautiful stained-glass windows and intricate religious tapestries, while the King's Apartments have a splendid mural of Alexander the Great, painted by Antonio Verrio. The Queen's Apartments and Georgian Rooms feature similarly elaborate paintings, chandeliers and tapestries. Listen out for the ghost of Catherine Howard – Henry's fifth wife, executed for adultery in 1542 – shrieking in the Haunted Gallery, or explore the Tudor Kitchens: their giant cauldrons and smoke-blackened fireplaces are regularly brought to life with cookery demonstrations, using centuries-old recipes.

Outside, the exquisitely landscaped gardens feature superb topiary, an ancient vine, peaceful Thames views, a reconstruction of a 16th-century heraldic garden and the famous Hampton Court maze.

East Molesey, Surrey KT8 9AU (0844 482 7777, www.hrp.org.uk). Hampton Court rail, or riverboat from Westminster or Richmond to Hampton Court Pier (Apr-Oct).

69 Madame Tussauds

There are some 300 waxwork figures in the collection, divided into zones. The A-list Party zone features Brad Pitt and Kate Moss, among others, while Sports has Muhammad Ali and Wayne Rooney; new arrivals include Benedict Cumberbatch. In addition to getting snapped with the stars, you can score a penalty goal or test your driving reactions using fun interactives. Other zones introduce you to film, pop and TV celebs, while the Scream attraction uses every special effect in the book, including floor drops, to make you quiver. Book online to avoid the enormous main queue and to save on the steep admission prices.

Marylebone Road, NW1 5LR (0871 894 3000, www.madame tussauds.com/london). Baker Street tube.

The British Library isn't just for scholars. Up the stairs to the left of the main entrance (be prepared to open your bags for the tiresome but necessary security check) is a room of bookish treasures. The free, changing display in the John Ritblat Gallery combines extraordinary historical artefacts – the Magna Carta, perhaps, with its cascade of wax seals, or a priceless Shakespeare First Folio – with such curios as handwritten lyrics from the Beatles or a 13-century Buddhist sutra. You sometimes have to pay for the impressive temporary exhibitions; the small but perfectly formed displays of the Folio Gallery are free.

96 Euston Road, NW1 2DB (0330 333 1144, www.bl.uk).
Euston or King's Cross tube/rail.

71 Splash out at London's department stores

While lesser shops come and go, the bastions of London's shopping scene remain its mighty department stores, which battle for shoppers' affections with all manner of retail thrills. **Liberty** (Regent Street, W1B 5AH, 7734 1234, www.liberty.co.uk; pictured) pairs sweetly old-fashioned premises with cutting-edge fashion: Erdem, Sessùn and APC are among the labels; exclusive designer collaborations abound; and accessories run from vertiginous Manolo Blahnik heels to classic Liberty-print diaries.

Selfridges (400 Oxford Street, W1A 1AB, 0800 123 4000, www. selfridges.com) is another fashionista favourite, famed for its extravagant window installations: Santa on a scooter, a Mad Hatter's tea party and a herd of galloping zebras have all featured in the past. Inside, delights include the extraordinary Shoe Galleries, which showcase over 4,000 shoes in a series of sumptuous boutiques. Innovative pop-ups and store-wide themed events keep shoppers on their toes, and there's even a permanent cinema.

Over in Knightsbridge, doormen in peaked caps open the doors into **Harrods** (87-135 Brompton Road, SW1X 7XL, 7730 1234, www.harrods. com), awash with marble, gilt sphinxes and ladies with poodles. But beyond the ostentation there's some seriously good shopping: the lingerie department stocks gorgeous pieces from the likes of Nina Ricci and Agent Provocateur; the Denim Lounge is chock-full of hip brands; and the shoe department – a whole floor, no less – claims to be the biggest in the world. On the ground floor, the food hall is a cornucopia of delicacies, and Ladurée's tearoom is as exquisite as its famous macaroons. A stone's throw away, **Harvey Nichols** (109-125 Knightsbridge, SW1X 7RJ, 7235 5000, www. harveynichols.com) offers polished service and eight floors of beauty, fashion, homewares and food. Don't miss the concept store-inspired fourth floor, which mixes pieces by emerging British designers with vintage magazines, cult toys and the 'Sneaker Wall' showcasing designs by Christian Louboutin, Beatrix Ong and other big names.

More down to earth than its rivals, **John Lewis** (300 Oxford Street, W1A 1EX, 7629 7711, www.johnlewis.com) remains dear to Londoners' hearts. Kitchenware, white goods and haberdashery are among its traditional strengths, although its fashion and beauty collections have become more directional of late. It's now looking smarter than ever, thanks to a multi-million-pound revamp that includes an impressive new beauty hall on the ground floor.

Imagine a museum free of children that can be explored with a glass of wine in hand. Over the last few years, special Lates events have enabled visitors to do just that, and have become a monthly (or sometimes weekly) fixture at many of London's finest museums and galleries. The format is similar whether you're at the National Gallery or the Museum of London (pictured), with a programme – often themed to tie in with the current blockbuster exhibition – combining DJs or live music, talks, perhaps a film screening, certainly a pay bar, and reduced ticket prices.

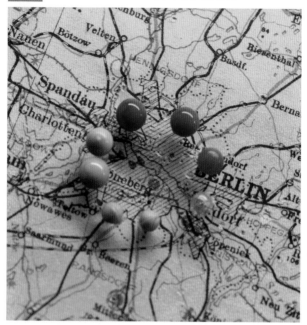

This cramped subterranean bunker was where Winston Churchill plotted Allied strategy in World War II, out of reach of the German bombers. Sealed off on 16 August 1945, its rooms exist in a state of suspended animation under the feet of Whitehall's shuffling bureaucrats. Every pin stuck into the vast charts was placed there in the final days of the conflict, as Churchill planned the end game to the war. Open to the public since 1984, the bunker powerfully brings to life the reality of a nation at war, with plenty of information on Churchill and his rousing speeches.
Clive Steps, King Charles Street, SW1A 2AQ (7930 6961, www.iwm.org.uk/visits/churchill-war-rooms). Westminster tube.

74 Hunterian Museum

Now displayed in ultra-modern, backlit glass cabinets, 18th-century anatomist John Hunter's vast collection of medical specimens is mind-bogglingly macabre. Diseased body parts, a two-tailed lizard, the skull of a two-headed boy and a set of premature quintuplets dating from 1786 are among the exhibits, along with Sir Winston Churchill's dentures. *Royal College of Surgeons, 35-43 Lincoln's Inn Fields, WC2A 3PE (7869 6560, www.hunterianmuseum.org). Holborn tube.*

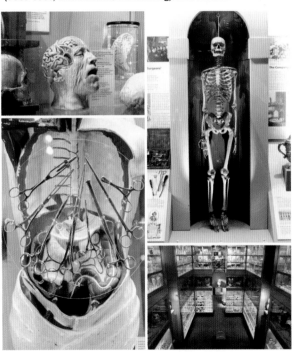

75 | The Tates

Connected by the River Thames, Tate Modern (pictured right) and Tate Britain (below) are two of the finest art galleries in the country. **Tate Britain** (Millbank, SW1P 4RG, 7887 8888, www.tate.org.uk) is the original – its stately Portland stone building has looked out over the Thames near Pimlico tube since 1897. Exhibits include a superb gallery of Turners, as well as works by Hogarth, Constable, Lucian Freud, Francis Bacon and other luminaries of British art.

Tate Modern (Bankside, SE1 9TG, 7887 8888, www.tate.org.uk) is the more high-profile – and busier.

It opened in a bold conversion of a riverside power station in 2000, and has been immensely popular ever since – so much so that an ambitious new extension is due to open in 2016. Covering every significant international movement of 20th-century art in its permanent collections, it also has changing installations in the vast turbine hall.

Admission to both Tates is free, but their blockbuster temporary exhibitions usually charge an entry fee. Great gift shops too.

76 | Covent Garden

This longtime tourist favourite has recently begun to draw in the locals too. Some impeccably cool shopping options have arrived (including a huge Apple Store, beauty boutique Aesop and sports/fashionwear specialist Y-3), while the street entertainers that perform around the historic covered market building, especially under the portico of St Paul's church, hold the crowds enthralled. For more on the area's attractions and upcoming events, have a look at www.coventgardenlondonuk.com.

▶ *Trams, horse-drawn buses and resplendent double-deckers are part of the collection at the London Transport Museum; see no.93.*

77 Horse Guards Parade & the Changing of the Guard

A short walk south of Trafalgar Square, an unsmiling young sentry under a shiny helmet is sitting atop a mighty horse. Welcome to Horse Guards – a stunning example of London's talent for military pageantry. Every morning at 11am (10am on Sundays), in the Parade Ground on the St James's Park side, the Changing of the Guard is a stately display of synchronised riding and immaculate uniforms: scarlet coats, polished boots, sabres and cuirasses (breastplates).

Watching the parade is free, but to learn more about the Horse Guards, pay the admission charge to enter the fine little Household Cavalry Museum. Inside, as well as memorabilia and video diaries from the soldiers, there are glass screens that allow you to look into the stables and see the magnificent steeds being groomed.

On alternate days, the guard is also changed at nearby Buckingham Palace. Here, you'll see regiments of Foot Guards wearing tall bearskin hats; it tends to be more crowded than Horse Guards, though, and fences keep you at a distance from much of the action.

Horse Guards, Whitehall, SW1A 2AX (7930 3070, www.householdcavalrymuseum.co.uk). Westminster tube or Charing Cross tube/rail.

▶ *For more on visiting Buckingham Palace, see no.89.*

78 Regent's Park

St James's Park may be prettier, but the sheer size of Regent's Park (7298 2000, www.royalparks.org.uk) makes it wonderfully varied. On one side, there's a busy waterfowl pond and a boating lake with an island where herons nest; on the other, a lovely rose garden. Several areas are dedicated to formal and informal sport, while the Camden side of the park is home to family favourite ZSL London Zoo (see no.4). From May to September, the **Open Air Theatre** (0844 826 4242, www.openairtheatre.com) produces classic musicals and Shakespearean comedies.

79 Sadler's Wells

Sadler's Wells is London's most important space dedicated to contemporary dance, and one of the best places in the city to experience the art form. The work on show is rich and varied, from reworkings of classical ballet to abstract contemporary works, taking in hip hop, flamenco, tango and more.

Rosebery Avenue, EC1R 4TN (0844 412 4300, www.sadlerswells.com). Angel tube.

80 Westminster Abbey & the Houses of Parliament

Designated a UNESCO World Heritage Site, the collection of historic buildings around Parliament Square is undeniably impressive – regardless of how many times you've seen them in holiday snaps.

Westminster tube exits in the shadow of the 'Big Ben' clock tower (Big Ben is the name of the largest bell within, not the tower itself). From here, the intricately worked, tobacco-coloured buildings of the Houses of Parliament (Parliament Square, SW1A 0AA, 7219 4272 Commons information, 7219 3107 Lords information, www.parliament.uk) march away south along the Thames until they reach Victoria Tower Gardens,

which has several interesting monuments (Rodin's *The Burghers of Calais*, a statue of suffragette Emmeline Pankhurst and the gaily coloured Buxton Memorial Fountain to the Emancipation of the Slaves). Parliament was extensively remodelled in the 1840s, but Westminster Hall retains its magnificent 14th-century hammer-beam roof; the only way to see it is to take one of the tours that run during Parliament's summer recess.

The south side of Parliament Square is dominated by the flying buttresses of Westminster Abbey (20 Dean's Yard, SW1P 3PA, 7222 5152 information, 7654 4900 tours, www.westminster-abbey.org), within which almost every English monarch has been crowned since the 11th century. Elizabeth I and Mary, Queen of Scots, are buried here, and Poets' Corner commemorates writers as varied as Tennyson, Henry James, Charles Dickens and Dylan Thomas.

81 Sample the Camden scene

It's hard not to feel a tad intoxicated by Camden's hedonistic, gleefully scruffy charms and air of rock 'n' roll excess. At its northern end, both the **Barfly** (49 Chalk Farm Road, NW1 8AN, 7688 8994, www.mamacolive.com/thebarfly; left) and the **Enterprise** (2 Haverstock Hill, NW3 2BL, 7485 2659, camdenenterprise.com offer a packed roster of up-and-coming rock and indie bands: the Strokes and Franz Ferdinand played early shows at the Barfly. Nearby, on Chalk Farm Road, the **Roundhouse** (0300 678 9222, www.roundhouse.org.uk; top) is a converted railway-engine shed with a bustling arts and music timetable of big-name alternative bands, top DJs, singer-songwriters, opera and theatre. Further south, the self-consciously cool **Lock Tavern** (35 Chalk Farm Road, NW1 8AJ, 7482

7163, www.lock-tavern.com) is frequented by clubbers, underground DJs and experimental bands. More DJ nights and cabaret are offered at **Proud Camden** (Stables Market, NW1 8AH, 7482 3867, www.proudcamden. com), a former horse hospital that's been converted into a quirky bar, gallery and venue. Reliable rock pub the **Hawley Arms** (2 Castlehaven Road, NW1 8QU, 7428 5979, www.thehawleyarms.co.uk; below), formerly a favourite of Amy Winehouse, sits just before the canal.

Heading into Camden proper, there are myriad pubs and music venues, including the slick **Jazz Café** (5-7 Parkway, NW1 7PG, 7485 6834, www.mamacolive.com/thejazzcafe), offering hip hop and soul alongside modern jazz; vegetarian café/folk music venue **Green Note** (106 Parkway, NW1 7AN, 7485 9899, www.greennote.co.uk); and the **Edinboro Castle** gastropub (57 Mornington Terrace, NW1 7RU, 7255 9651, www.edinborocastlepub.co.uk) with its top-notch beer garden. The **Dublin Castle** (94 Parkway, NW1 7AN, 7485 1773, www.thedublincastle. com) is rich in musical history (Blur, the Killers and Coldplay have all performed here); it's a little beer-sodden and grimy, but good for cheap pints and noisy gigs. Backstreet boozer the **Black Heart** (3 Greenland Place, NW1 0AP, 7428 9730, www.ourblackheart.com) has a buzzy, New York dive-bar vibe, while opposite Mornington Crescent tube lies former music hall **Koko** (1A Camden High Street, NW1 7JE, 7388 3222, www. koko.uk.com), a heaving venue that hosts everyone from Kasabian to Gilles Peterson.

The one-day **Camden Rocks Festival** (www.camdenrocksfestival.com), at the end of May, offers an eardrum-battering mix of hard rock, metal and alternative indie bands; perfect for those who like their music live, loud and lewd.

▶ *In the daytime, Camden Market (see no.37) is the big draw. It's great for people-watching, even if you don't make any purchases.*

82 | Trafalgar Square

Laid out in the 1820s and named in honour of Nelson's famous naval victory, this majestic square is the heart of modern London. Above it soars Nelson's Column, topped with a statue of the valiant vice admiral – often with a disrespectful pigeon perched upon his head. Far below Nelson's lofty gaze, three lower plinths are occupied by statues of George IV and Victorian military heroes. The fourth plinth is given over to temporary art installations. Featured artists have included Mark Quinn,

Katharina Fritsch and Antony Gormley, whose *One & Other* invited 2,400 members of the public to stand atop the plinth for an hour.

The square is both a place of protest and of celebration; on 8 May 1945, huge crowds gathered here to listen to Churchill's broadcast announcing victory in Europe. Throughout the year, a busy programme of events features food stalls, music, dancers and parades: in October or November, the Diwali festival of light is always spectacular, while Christmas brings carol singers and a towering Norwegian spruce, swathed in twinkling lights. For full details of what's on, visit www.london.gov.uk/priorities/arts-culture/trafalgar-square.

83 | Natural History Museum

Generations of children have stood in the soaring central hall here, gazing up at the enormous diplodocus (nicknamed 'Dippy' by staff). A more recent addition to the museum's prehistoric menagerie is its animatronic T-Rex, also on the ground floor, whose baleful eyes, swishing tail and throaty roars send younger visitors running for cover; and a new Stegosaurus skeleton. Smaller beasts are covered here too, though – not least the leaf-cutting ants of the Creepy Crawlies gallery, toiling away in an enormous, glass-walled formicary.

Exhibits in the geology-focused Red Zone include a ground-shaking earthquake simulator and chunks of moon rock, precious metals and glow-in-the-dark minerals, while the Orange Zone takes in a wildlife garden and the eight-storey Darwin Centre, which opened in 2009. The centre's vast, cocoon-shaped structure is a marvel in itself; venture inside to watch scientists at work in state-of-the-art laboratories and see some weird and wonderful plant and insect specimens.

Cromwell Road, SW7 5BD (7942 5000, www.nhm.ac.uk).
South Kensington tube.

Although admission prices are steep, children will delight in this five-floor 'odditorium', which is devoted to all things strange, spooky and downright freaky. A two-headed calf and a shark jaw vie for visitors' attention with medieval torture devices and a smoking reconstruction of an electric chair; less grisly oddities include a statue of the Beatles made from chewing gum, a life-size Ferrari made of wool, Marilyn Monroe's make-up bag and Leonardo's *Last Supper*, painted on a grain of rice. Tackle the Vortex – a giddying contraption involving a bridge and a spinning kaleidoscope – at your peril, and preferably before having lunch.
1 Piccadilly Circus, W1J 0DA (3238 0022,
www.ripleyslondon.com). Piccadilly Circus tube.

Newer arrivals may have fancier dining rooms and smoother service, but the bold Mediterranean flavours and hefty portions at London's first gastropub, the **Eagle** (159 Farringdon Road, EC1R 3AL, 7837 1353, www.theeaglefarringdon.com; pictured above), mean it remains a firm favourite. With its mismatched wooden chairs, tumblers of red wine and pared-down menu, Southwark's **Anchor & Hope** (36 The Cut, SE1 8LP, 7928 9898, www.anchorandhopepub.co.uk) has a similarly casual vibe – and is only a short walk from Tate Modern (see no.75). You

can't book, so there's often a wait in the bar before you can squeeze on to one of the communal tables and order up a feast: a rich, wintry cassoulet, perhaps, or cod and lentils with green sauce.

In the heart of the East End, the **Culpeper** (40 Commercial Street, E1 6LP, 7247 5371, www. theculpeper.com; pictured right) is a handsome Victorian inn, lovingly updated. Food is unfussy and simply presented, with a focus on flavour – a proper ploughman's, say, or grilled sardines – while drinks include London craft beers.

Over the last decade, brothers Tom and Ed Martin have built up a set of excellent gastropubs. One of their first was the **Gun** (27 Coldharbour, E14 9NS, 7515 5222, www.thegundocklands. com), on the Isle of Dogs. It stands across the river from the O2 arena (see no.42), with great views from its terrace. The food is British and hearty: think Isle of Man scallops, followed by roast partridge with stuffed cabbage. They also run the **Jugged Hare** (49 Chiswell Street, EC1Y 4SA, 7614 0134, www.thejuggedhare.com), which is handy for the Barbican (no.40).

Head west to Fulham for the upmarket **Harwood Arms** (Walham Grove, SW6 1QP, 7386 1847, www. harwoodarms.com), which gained a Michelin star in 2010. Getting a table isn't easy, but persevere for dishes such as T-bone of Berkshire fallow deer with pickled beetroot or the signature snails with stout-braised oxtail and bone marrow.

86 Royal Academy of Arts

The grand, Palladian Burlington House makes a suitably dignified setting for the Royal Academy's headquarters. Free-entry shows run alongside ticketed blockbuster exhibitions, while the biggest event of the year remains the Summer Exhibition – a fixture since 1769. Works by illustrious Royal Academians (including the likes of David Hockney and Sarah Lucas) are shown alongside submissions by the general public; most are for sale, with prices starting from around £75 and climbing into six figures for the star pieces.

Burlington House, Piccadilly, W1J 0BD (7300 8000, www.royal academy.org.uk). Green Park or Piccadilly Circus tube.

87 Highgate Cemetery

Opened in 1839, not long after Queen Victoria came to the throne, Highgate Cemetery is superbly atmospheric with its crumbling Gothic monuments, blank-eyed angels and trailing ivy. The East Cemetery is open to the public daily (except when there is a burial) and contains the monument to Karl Marx, as well as the remains of novelists George Eliot and Douglas Adams; the West Cemetery is prettier, but can only be visited on a tour (children under eight are not allowed). Other famous occupants include physicist Michael Faraday, murdered Russian dissident Alexander Litvinenko, punk impresario Malcolm McLaren and a gaggle of Pre-Raphaelites – among them poet Christina Rossetti and Elizabeth Siddal, model for John Everett Millais' *Ophelia*.

Swain's Lane, N6 6PJ (8340 1834, www.highgatecemetery.org). Archway tube.

88 Lord's Cricket Ground

A sleepy summer's day at the spiritual home of cricket is one of London's sporting treats. The stadium is a surprisingly harmonious marriage of old and new, combining a gracious red-brick Victorian pavilion and the futuristic white pod that houses the Media Centre. Tickets for international fixtures – whether the five-day Test matches beloved of connoisseurs, a single-day 50-over-a-side match or the crash-bang-wallop excitement of a three-hour Twenty20 contest – are hard to come by unless you book

well in advance. Better instead to attend domestic fixtures (this is the home ground of the Middlesex County Cricket Club) or book a place on one of the guided tours around the buildings and the MCC Museum. Memorabilia on display runs from the game's most famous trophy – the tiny Ashes urn – and portraits of WG Grace to a stuffed sparrow, attached to the cricket ball that killed it in 1936. Tours are held daily except on match days and are very popular, so book well ahead.

St John's Wood Road, NW8 8QN (7616 8500, www.lords.org).
St John's Wood tube.

To find out whether Her Majesty is in residence, check which flag is fluttering above the palace: if it's the Royal Standard rather than the Union Jack, she's at home. In August and September, she won't be. That's when the Queen visits Scotland – and the palace's 19 sumptuously appointed State Rooms are opened to the public.

For the rest of the year, admire family heirlooms in the Queen's Gallery, which contains paintings by Rubens and Rembrandt and some exquisite Sèvres porcelain (George IV was a keen collector), or head to the Royal

Mews to see the royal fleet of Bentleys and Rolls-Royces, along with the splendid carriages and the horses that pull them (the names of the Windsor greys are chosen by the Queen).

The Mall, SW1A 1AA (7766 7300, www.royalcollection. org.uk). Green Park tube or Victoria tube/rail.

▶ *For a burst of regal pomp and ceremony, join the crowds that gather to watch the Changing of the Guard; see no.77.*

90 Saatchi Gallery

A champion of the headline-grabbing Young British Artists of the 1990s (notably Damien Hirst and Tracey Emin), Charles Saatchi remains a prodigious collector of contemporary art. Set in a huge converted military barracks just off the King's Road in Chelsea, the Saatchi Gallery showcases global art rather than focusing on the Brits. Changing exhibitions of contemporary art occupy its minimalist, white-painted galleries, featuring paintings and sculptures by both big names and lesser-known talents. Look out too for longstanding favourites such as *20:50*, Richard Wilson's deceptively simple and visually spectacular sump-oil installation. Entry is free.

Duke of York's HQ, off King's Road, SW3 4SQ (7811 3081, www.saatchi-gallery.co.uk). Sloane Square tube.

Half the fun of a day out in Greenwich is getting there. Although you can catch the DLR, it's more exciting to take a Thames Clipper (see no.15) and disembark at Greenwich Pier, by the **Cutty Sark** (King William Walk, SE10 9HT, 8312 6608, www.rmg.co.uk). This 19th-century tea clipper, once the fastest ship in the world, emerged in 2012 after a massive renovation project. It's been raised above the ground so visitors can admire the hull from underneath.

After a meander through the stalls and shops of **Greenwich Market**, head for the free-entry Discover Greenwich exhibition, set in the corner of the **Old Royal Naval College** (2 Cutty Sark Gardens, SE10 9LW, 8269 4747, www.ornc.org) nearest the *Cutty Sark*. Artefacts and exhibits explore the area's rich history and imposing architecture (not for nothing is Greenwich a UNESCO World Heritage Site), while children can build their own grand designs in soft bricks or try to lift a knight's jousting lance. The Naval College's other highlight is the splendid ceiling of the Painted Hall, which took Sir James Thornhill almost two decades to complete.

The vast white colonnades of the Naval College – which seem to shimmer when the sun is bright – were designed by Sir Christopher Wren to frame Inigo Jones's much more modest **Queen's House**, across the Romney Road. Completed in 1638, the house has an intriguing collection of seafaring art and a splendid interior court, tiled in black and white. It's run by the neighbouring **National Maritime Museum** (Park Row, SE10 9NF, 8858 4422, www.rmg. co.uk), whose immense collection of maritime maps, instruments and regalia includes the blood-stained coat in which Nelson met his end. The Voyagers gallery, in the new Sammy Ofer wing, is a good introduction to the museum. There's interactive fun to be had exploring the Great Map, and in the Children's Gallery, where you can load cargo, steer a ferry into port and fire a cannon at pirates.

Behind the museum stretches **Greenwich Park**. It's a steep ten-minute hike across the park and up to the **Royal Observatory** (8858 4422, www.rmg.co.uk), although there is also a shuttle bus. At the top, you can straddle the Prime Meridian Line, marked on the courtyard's flagstones, then check out the 14th-century timekeeping equipment and 28-inch refracting telescope in Flamsteed House, built in 1675 for the first Astronomer Royal, Sir John Flamsteed. In addition, you can take in a spectacular star-show in the Peter Harrison Planetarium (pictured below) before re-emerging, blinking, into the daylight.

92 See a West End show

For a night of theatrical glitz and glamour, the West End is still the place to go, with numerous big-budget shows running year-round. Productions change, of course, but you'll always find extravagant musical versions of blockbuster films, such as the touching *Billy Elliot the Musical*. Then there are the 'jukebox' musicals, with narratives constructed around hit songs (the thoroughly enjoyable *Jersey Boys*, for example, which traces the career of Frankie Valli and the Four Seasons) and the 'proper' musicals, which include the lavish, long-running *Les Misérables*.

If ticket prices seem off-puttingly high, pay a visit to **Tkts** (Clocktower Building, WC2H 7NA, www.tkts.co.uk), which occupies a stand-alone booth on the south side of Leicester Square. Operated by the Society of London Theatre, it sells tickets for many of the big shows at much-reduced rates, either on the day or up to a week in advance. Many West End theatres also offer standby seats (their own reduced-price tickets for shows that haven't sold out on the night).

The West End's lavish productions are, of course, just one side of London's thriving theatre scene. For new plays and rising talents, head for

Chelsea's famously radical **Royal Court Theatre** (Sloane Square, SW1W 8AS, 7565 5000, www.royalcourttheatre.com); in recent years, several productions have transferred from its modest stage to the West End and beyond.

In Covent Garden, the **Donmar Warehouse** (41 Earlham Street, WC2H 9LX, 0844 871 7624, www.donmarwarehouse.com) is another place to catch shows before they hit the big time – and to see Hollywood stars such as Nicole Kidman and Gwyneth Paltrow honing their craft on its tiny stage. Meanwhile, Kevin Spacey's role as artistic director (until autumn 2015) at the **Old Vic** (The Cut, SE1 8NB, 0844 871 7628, www.oldvictheatre.com) ensures a sprinkling of big-name stars at this grand Victorian theatre.

93 London Transport Museum

A gleaming collection of vehicles – running from a jaunty little horse-drawn tram to increasingly sleek variations on the classic red bus – brings the city's transport history to life. The collection of posters is superb too, extolling Londoners to see the sights, do their Christmas shopping, join the war effort and say 'please' and 'thank you' to London Underground staff; look out for a surreal design by Man Ray, dating from the 1930s. *Covent Garden Piazza, WC2E 7BB (7379 6344, www.ltmuseum.co.uk). Covent Garden tube.*

94 Sip a cocktail

At cosy **Dukes Bar** (Dukes Hotel, 35 St James's Place, SW1A 1NY, 7491 4840, www.dukeshotel.com), three small rooms decorated like a country-house drawing room provide some of London's finest cocktails, including super-strong martinis made at your table. Other classic hotel cocktail dens are the art deco **American Bar** at the Savoy (100 Strand, WC2R 0EW, 7836 4343, www.fairmont.com/savoy-london), little changed since its 1920s heyday, and the **Connaught Bar** (16 Carlos Place, W1K 2AL, 7499 7070, www.the-connaught.com), part of the equally swish Connaught hotel, with its sumptuous, '20s-influenced decor.

The city is also renowned for innovation and experimentation, and one of the boldest proponents is drinks maestro Tony Conigliaro. You can sample his alchemical wizardry at **69 Colebrooke Row** (69 Colebrooke Row, N1 8AA, 07540 528593, www.69colebrookerow.com; pictured), tucked away on an Islington backstreet. The premises are tiny, so it's advisable to reserve a table. Conigliaro is also behind the cocktail lists at the **Zetter Townhouse** (49-50 St John's Square, EC1V 4JJ, 7324 4545, www.thezettertownhouse.com), on the ground floor of a hip Clerkenwell hotel; and tiny **Bar Termini** (7 Old Compton Street, W1D 5JE, 07680 945018, www.bar-termini.com), in the heart of Soho.

Several of the best cocktail spots are located in atmospheric basements, often with a 'speakeasy' feel. **Purl** (50 Blandford Street, W1U 7HX, 7935 0835, www.purl-london.com), a Marylebone veteran, features low lighting, leather chesterfields, great jazz on the sound system and a laid-back, inviting vibe. In Shoreditch, spacious, award-winning **Nightjar** (129 City Road, EC1V 1JB, 7253 4101, www.barnightjar.com) has a stunning pressed-tin ceiling and a fabulous historical cocktail menu that runs from pre-Prohibition to the present.

95 | Sea Life London Aquarium

All aquatic life is here, from jauntily striped clown fish to endangered Cuban crocodiles. Starfish, crabs and anemones can be handled in special open rock pools, while the Shark Walk – they swim beneath your feet – provides a delicious frisson of danger. Book online (and for slots after 3pm) for cheaper tickets.

County Hall, Riverside Building, Westminster Bridge Road, SE1 7PB (0871 663 1678, www.visitsealife.co.uk/london). Westminster tube or Waterloo tube/rail.

96 | Wellcome Collection

This wonderfully offbeat museum is based around the medical curios collected by globe-trotting 19th-century pharmacist Sir Henry Wellcome. His fascinating and often macabre finds include ivory carvings of pregnant women, used guillotine blades, Napoleon's toothbrush and a Chinese torture chair. The museum also examines modern medical matters with the help of attention-grabbing contemporary art. Downstairs is a bookshop, a café and a space for the excellent temporary exhibitions. Themes such as recreational drugs ('High Society') and human sexuality ('The Institute of Sexology') are always entertainingly explored, with associated special events that might include lectures, gigs, operettas and experiments. The museum has proved so popular that it's expanding to create much-needed additional exhibition space, plus a new restaurant and a showpiece spiral staircase.

183 Euston Road, NW1 2BE (7611 2222, www.wellcome collection.org). Euston Square tube or Euston tube/rail.

97 Columbia Road Market

On a Sunday morning (8am-3pm), this fragrant East End flower market is a lovely place to be. The street becomes a sea of blooms, packed with vibrant hothouse beauties, sweet-smelling stocks and bargain-priced bedding plants ('three for a fiver' is the stallholders' rallying cry).

Galleries and boutiques also thrive here. Scents specialist **Angela Flanders** (96 Columbia Road, E2 7QB, 7739 7555, www.angelaflanders-perfumer.com) is one of the longest-established shops. **Choosing Keeping** (no.128, E2 7RG, 7613 3842, www.choosingkeeping.com) caters for stationery fans with its loving curated pens, scissors and notebooks, while next door, at no.126, the charming **Ryantown** (7613 1510, www.robryanstudio.co.uk) is where artist Rob Ryan sells his intricate cut-paper artworks, screenprints and other gifts. Don't miss the only café of subversive baker **Lily Vanilli** (6 The Courtyard, Ezra Street, E2 7RH, www.lilyvanilli.com) – made famous by her bleeding heart cakes. *Columbia Road, E2 (www.columbiaroad.info). Hoxton rail or Liverpool Street tube/rail then bus 26, 48.*

▶ *It's a short walk to the delights of Brick Lane (see no.47).*

98 | Royal Opera House

The Royal Opera and the Royal Ballet are both based at this soaring 19th-century opera house, making for a packed cultural programme. Meanwhile, daily backstage tours offer a peek behind the scenes – if you're lucky, you might catch members of the Royal Ballet practising their pirouettes. Otherwise, look out over the bustle of Covent Garden from the covered loggia of the Amphitheatre restaurant-bar, open from spring each year.

Covent Garden, WC2E 9DD (7240 1200, www.roh.org.uk).
Covent Garden tube.

99 | Notting Hill Carnival

For three days over the August bank holiday weekend, the streets of Notting Hill are taken over by Europe's largest street party, attended by over a million revellers. Steel bands, pounding sound systems, Caribbean food stalls and plenty of rum punch are all thrown into the mix, while stilt-walkers, fabulous costumes, shimmying dancers and a generous quantity of sequins make the parades (the children's parade is held on Sunday, the adults' on Monday) a sight to remember.
www.thenottinghillcarnival.com.

100 Open House London

For one weekend each September, Open House London allows visitors a glimpse inside hundreds of buildings that are normally out of bounds to the public. It's a hugely – and deservedly – popular event: if the glass and steel Lloyd's of London building is taking part, it usually has a queue snaking all along Leadenhall Street by mid morning, while the number of visitors for the very rarest openings (such as the BT Tower) is controlled by a ticket ballot. Buildings might run from the former Fleet Street headquarters of the *Daily Express* (a sleek, black, art deco masterpiece) to the members-only London Library in St James's Square, along with Hindu temples, eco-friendly private abodes, state-of-the-art skyscrapers and dusty churches. No matter how well you know the city, there's always a corner still to explore – which is why we love this event. ***www.londonopenhouse.org.***

Central London

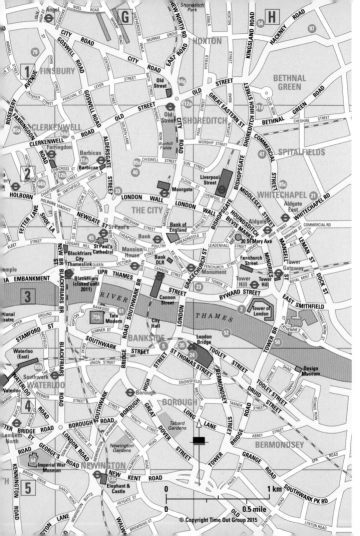

Venues in grey either lie off the map or can't be plotted (for example, fireworks displays). Bullet numbers correspond to the order in which venues appear in the book, not the page number.

A-Z Index

By Area